**foreword by Carl R. Boyd**

# donna o. johnson & y.c. chen

follow our 3-step plan and
if you don't make all A's, ***we will give you $100***

# guaranteed
# A+
## plus  2nd Edition!

secrets to higher grades and less study time
for high school students

Cover: Alpha Advertising (www.alphaadvertising.com)
Layout: Pine Hill Graphics (www.pinehillgraphics.com)

Published by:
JCYC Studio
Dallas, Texas
www.JCYCStudio.com

*In Cooperation with*
**Guaranteed 4.0 Learning System, LLC**
*17194 Preston Road, Suite 102*
*Mail Code 338*
*Dallas, TX 75248*
*www.NoMoreStudy.com*

**Guaranteed 4.0 Companion Workbook**
Copyright ©2005 Donna O. Johnson, Y.C. Chen
All rights reserved

Cover Design by Alpha Advertising
Interior Design by Pine Hill Graphics

Packaged by Pine Hill Graphics

Publisher's Cataloging-in-Publication Data
*(Provided by Cassidy Cataloguing Services, Inc.)*

Johnson, Donna O.

    Guaranteed A+ plus : secrets to higher grades and less study time
for high school students / Donna O. Johnson & Y. C. Chen ;
foreword by Carl R. Boyd. -- 2nd ed. -- Dallas, TX : JCYC Studio,
2008.

    p. ; cm.

    ISBN: 978-0-9742648-4-4
    Audience: high school students.
    "Follow our 3-step plan and if you don't make all A's, we will
give you $100."

    1. Study skills--United States--Programmed instruction. 2. High
school students--Time management--United States. 3. Education,
Secondary--United States. 4. College preparation programs--
United States. I. Chen, Y. C. (Ya-Chin) II. Title. III. Guaranteed A
plus.

LB2395.4 .J639 2008
371.3/0281--dc22          0801

# Table of Contents

✦ ✦ ✦ ✦ ✦ ✦ ✦ ✦ ✦ ✦ ✦ ✦ ✦ ✦ ✦ ✦ ✦

*School, 2 Million Dollars & Your Dreams!*
*Pay yourself (Big Money) with your Brain*

**Tips to get the most out of this book**

## Part I: Donna O.'s Guaranteed 4.0 Plan

*What is stress?*
*Is it normal?*
*How can I manage stress?*
*Chapter I Review*

*WHAT to do vs. HOW to do it*
*What do you do every week?*
*Guaranteed A+ PLUS Time Management Principles*
*Chapter II Review*

Why should you go?
Where should I sit?
Why should you sit there?
Step 1 Review
TOH - Why & When?
3 secrets about your teachers
Step 2 Review
Section 3.1
What to do before going to class?
Do you remember what you read?
Bullet Point Reading (BPR)
BPR Examples
Section Review - 3.1

## Part 2: Applying the 4.0 Plan—A Student's Perspective

# Foreword

## Carl R. Boyd, Advice Teacher

The Lord has blessed me to have kind people in my life. My wife, "Wonderful Wanda," and her family are kind people. My family is comprised of kind people. My church family, and professional colleagues are, often, quite kind. I felt that Donna O. Johnson and Y.C. Chen were being kind when they invited me to write the foreword for this very important book. Indeed, they are kind people; good folk; God's Lights.

This, however, is not a testimonial. The thought, re: kindness, occurred to me as I realized that the principles from A+ are as helpful to me in my own ministry, working with teachers, as they have been to college students (Guaranteed 4.0, Copyright 2004); and will most certainly be, through this manual, to secondary students everywhere. I thought, "how kind of them to give me this tool." Especially helpful are the concepts dealing with time management, devoting 100% to my tasks and using the BP notebook.

Beginning with providing real reasons for learning (many bright students are simply unmotivated and, thus, unsuccessful), then offering practical approaches towards attaining optimal achievement, Donna O. Johnson provides a tremendous help to classroom teachers. They continually seek ways to make subject matter relevant to students' lives. Additionally, educators want students to employ thinking skills. This book begins with thought-provoking questions which make the pursuit of learning relevant to students' aspirations.

For students, Donna O. Johnson is today's students' "Mama Pearle" (see 3 Secrets). If they adhere to her methods, as she adhered to her grandmother's mantra, they are likely to be as successful as she. No, they are GUARANTEED to be, even more so. Considering that, after four decades as an educator—having begun as a 7/8 science teacher in Chicago's Public Schools in 1964—I am, now, using the principles from this work, I can say, without equivocation, that this book will be useful for a lifetime. Sometime in the future—more likely the near than the distant—many students, seeing significant improvement because of Donna O. Johnson and Y.C. Chen's writing, will be saying to themselves, and others, "How kind of them to give us this tool."

The Lord has blessed us to have nice—and, very helpful—people in our lives.

# Acknowledgments

+ + + + ◆ ◆ ◆ ◆ ◆ ◆ ◆ + + + +

With our hearts in awe, we first give honor to God for who He is. He opened our eyes so we can help others to unlock their God-given potential. He is the divine inspiration for the creativity behind our work. He is the giver of hope who empowers us to forge ahead regardless of circumstances. He endowed us with His wisdom, knowledge and understanding to enable us to fulfill the call on our lives. He sends family, friends, colleagues and loved ones as traveling companions in this journey.

Indeed, we honor God for who He is and for what He has done in our lives.

We also want to acknowledge our families who have supported us throughout the years. A very special appreciation goes to our high school teachers from Center, Texas and San Jose, California who are simply exceptional educators. We are forever grateful for those 4.0 administrators, students, parents and friends who encouraged us and gave their valuable time and advice. We especially want to thank the following people who are most directly responsible for this book becoming a reality:

Betty Crawford, Pastors Brian & Sabrina Holmes, Cal Walker, Carl Boyd, Clif & Carol King, Debbie Morris, Judge Dianne Jones, Col. & Mrs. Donald Jones, Sr., Mr. & Mrs. Hezekiah Hawkins, Dr. Howard Adams, Janis Moore, Joan Robinson-Berry, Pastor John van Niekerk, Jose Rivera, Dr. Joyce Brown, Bishop Joseph & Pastor Barbara Garlington, Dr. Joy Vann-Hamilton, Dr. Kaye Jeter, Dr. Kent Wallace, Dr. Lee Noel, Madeline Powell, Marieta Julean, Mike Cox, Myrna Morrow, Neeka Jones, Oliver Dacey, Paulette Gaines, Rafaela Schwan, Raul Munoz, Mr. & Mrs. Richard Terry, Drs. Robert & Carolyn Smith, Pastor Sanford Cooper, Sharon Garrison, Mr. & Mrs. Stafford Braxton, Dr. Tamiko Youngblood, Dr. Tyrone Cushman, Pastor Vincent Manzo and Wanda Dennis.

# Introduction

✦ ✦ ✦ ✦ ✦ ✦ ✦ ✦ ✦ ✦ ✦ ✦ ✦ ✦ ✦ ✦

### *School, 2 Million Dollars & Your Dreams!*

The importance of education is not new. It has been emphasized since the times of the ancient Chinese, Greeks and Romans. Even now, many Hollywood movie stars, politicians and athletes talk about the importance of education, encouraging students to stay in school. Education is a non-stop topic of conversation on television, radio and of course, in our schools. If you are like other high school students across the country, you won't go through a week without noticing some form of the message that "SCHOOL IS IMPORTANT."

The truth is "SCHOOL IS IMPORTANT," and grades are important.

I believe most students want to make straight A's and they want to learn. However, many times, we have been told "What to do" but not the "How to" of doing it. Students often hear things like: "study harder," "focus more," and "you need to apply yourself." But how often is there really someone waiting in the wings to show you how to achieve your goals. As a student you could easily feel overwhelmed by different and sometimes conflicting advice. Sometimes it is hard to see the point of high school because the future seems so far away. But there is hope and a guaranteed plan that will help you!

**If your goal is to have good grades while reducing study time; you definitely need this plan!**

I empathize with you. That is why we are making the Guaranteed A+ Plus plan available to high school students. Yes, I can hear your mind clicking. You are thinking, how can anyone guarantee a student all A's? Well, it can be done. On our *"Guaranteed A+ Plus Learning System,"* any student can receive all A's. *In fact, I put my money where my mouth is and let the money do the talking.* Here is our famous $100 guarantee. Yes, you read correctly. The A+ PLUS Plan is guaranteed.

**If you follow the 3 basic steps of this program exactly and do not earn straight A's, we will give you one hundred dollars!**

Students in our seminars always want to know if we have ever paid the $100 guarantee. The answer is NEVER! This amazing "zero-casualty" record is not because we are cheap and tightfisted; it is because the program really does work! In 18+ years, we have presented this system to more than 1 million students, ranging from 5th graders to PhD candidates. Every student who has followed the plan has made straight A's!

Even students who started the plan after the school term began, showed drastic improvement in their grades. Many people have called or emailed to say "thank-you." But the most memorable and cherished experiences are those when parents have called while crying, telling us that their child is off academic probation and now on the Dean's List. Also, we constantly get e-mails, phone calls and postcards from students sharing their testimonies. It is a very rewarding job for me!

During the last 18+ years, we have had the opportunity to share this powerful learning system through live presentations across the country. And because of the success of the system, a friend, Y.C. Chen, convinced me to write a book so more college students could benefit from this program. This is actually our second book together. After such an overwhelming response from the first book, we decided that we had to also share the "Guaranteed A+ Plus System" in a book format so that more high school students could get better grades in less time!

✦ ✦ ✦ ✦ ✦ ✦ ✦ ✦ ✦ ✦

### Guaranteed A+ P.L.U.S.
### • <u>P</u>reparing <u>L</u>earners for <u>U</u>ltimate <u>S</u>uccess

✦ ✦ ✦ ✦ ✦ ✦ ✦ ✦ ✦ ✦

If you are a 12th grader or a college student, we recommend that you read our first book, Guaranteed 4.0, that was written specifically for college students. (Please see www.NoMoreStudy.com)

## *Pay yourself (Big Money) with your Brain*

Zero is a funny number. By itself, it means nothing, literally. But when I add 0's after another number, it has a multiplying / magnifying effect! For example, would you like to have $100 or would you like me to add four 0's to that number? Of course, you would want me to add four 0's and make it a "cool million"! Just how can you get a million dollars? I don't think we should bet on you winning a reality show like "Survivor" or "Fear Factor." (By the way, Fear Factor pays far less and you have to eat bugs or other disgusting things.) What if I tell you that you can pay yourself with your brain and make much more than a million dollars?

Again, it is not news when you are told to "get a good education so you can get a good paying job." However, it is usually a very vague concept to us. **Just how much are your grades and education worth?** We know that people who finish college make more than others who don't. But, just how much more money do they make? Allow me to show you some concrete numbers with this chart.

| Education Level | Did not finish High School | Finish High School | Finish College (Average GPA) |
|---|---|---|---|
| Average salary at Age 24 | $23,176 | $31,075 | $50,394 |

**When you finish College, you make almost $ 17,000 more than people who only finished high school!**

Maybe you are still skeptical; let's look at how well you can do over the course of your life time.

| Education Level | Did not finish High School | Finish High School | Finish College |
|---|---|---|---|
| Estimated Life time Earnings | $1.23 million | $1.79 million | $3.27 million |

You can pay yourself with your brain far more with a college degree than if you only finish high school. In fact, $2 million dollars more! If we average it over the course of your career, you will earn almost $47,000 more a year! In fact, **you would have worked fewer years and earned much more.** Now, do you want the $100 or the extra $2 million?

❖ ❖ ❖ ❖ ❖ ❖ ❖ ❖ ❖

### Very simply, education gives you choices.
### More education gives you more choices.

❖ ❖ ❖ ❖ ❖ ❖ ❖ ❖ ❖

Of course, money is not everything. Here is the bottom line: It is about choice. **Education gives you choices and quality education gives you more choices in life.** How would you like to choose to attend the college you desire? How about choosing from various scholarship offers? How about the ability to choose the career you like rather than settling for whatever jobs you can get? Let's look at even longer term. What kind of car would you like to drive? What kind of house would you like to live in? What kind of quality of life would you like to have?

In all honesty, I did not just go to school for money. You could, but your life is far bigger and more important than being satisfied with a good paying job. Money is simply a means to the end for what you love to do. Through education, you can have access to great opportunities and many rewarding experiences. After working as an engineer for a few years, I decided to own my own company so I could help more people. My education helped me to start and grow my business and I now have my dream job. Education is not all about money; it is about fulfilling the dreams God has placed in you. Dream big, aim high and quality education can take you there.

❖ ❖ ❖ ❖ ❖ ❖ ❖ ❖ ❖

### Education is not all about money;
### it is about fulfilling the dreams
### God has placed in you.

### Dream big, aim high, and
### quality education can take you there.

❖ ❖ ❖ ❖ ❖ ❖ ❖ ❖ ❖

Now, you might ask, "What makes the Guaranteed A+ Plus Learning System work?" The answer is truly simple: in addition to telling students "what to do," we show them "how to do it." It is a guaranteed proven method. The uniqueness of the program is that it is actually a system—a complete A to Z learning approach that is designed to eliminate frustration and trial-and-error. In essence, we take the mystery out of learning!

As you read this book, you may recognize many of the principles. In fact, you might even think: "This is common sense stuff!" While we have solid scientific research as the foundation of the program, we chose to present information in plain English and organized it in a way that was easy to digest. Therefore, whether you are an 8th grader getting ready for high school or a college-bound junior in the midst of SAT-prep, you can understand and follow the Guaranteed A+ Plus Plan. **The 3 main sections of the Guaranteed A+ PLUS Learning System are:**

### I. Stress Management

### II. Time Management

### III. The Guaranteed 3 Steps

Here is the bottom line:

1. It does not matter what your academic success has been; it only matters what you want to achieve. With the A+ PLUS Plan, your grades are guaranteed to improve!

2. If you can remember the ABC song, you can master the A+ PLUS Plan.

3. You have great potential. More education will give you more choices in life when you stay on the A+ PLUS Plan.

# Tips to get the most out of the Guaranteed A+ Plus Learning System

◆ ◆ ◆ ◆ ◆ ◆ ◆ ◆ ◆ ◆ ◆ ◆ ◆ ◆ ◆

**If you have the DVD/Video curriculum,**

- Fill out the workbook as you watch the curriculum

- Complete each Guaranteed A+ PLUS Exercise in the workbook and check it with the DVD or book's chapter review before continuing to the next section.

- Use this book as a reference after viewing each module on DVD/Video for more examples and detailed explanation if necessary

**If you don't have the DVD/Video curriculum,**

- Don't worry, the book is written such that the Guaranteed A+ PLUS Plan can be learned without the DVD/Video curriculum

- Read in a place where you can focus

  - a quiet place other than your bed

- Instead of highlighting, fill out the workbook as you read

- Complete each Guaranteed A+ PLUS Exercise in the workbook and check it with the book's chapter review before continuing to the next section.

If you would like to purchase the DVD/Video curriculum or additional workbooks, they are available at www.NoMoreStudy.com.

# Part 1

# Donna O's Guaranteed A+ PLUS Plan

## By Donna O. Johnson

Dedicated to Mildred E. Johnson, the best mother in the world. Words could never express my appreciation for the life you have prepared me to live. Thanks for dedicating your life to guiding and supporting your children after the death of our father James C. Johnson. Though a single mother since I was 19 months old, your strength and endurance provide the stability and security of a two parent home. Your faith in God, positive attitude and your smiles have been a constant reminder that I can do all things through Christ who strengthens me!

# Chapter I

+ + + + + + ◆ ◆ ◆ ◆ + + +

# *Stress Management*

The first chapter of this book is about **stress management**! One might ask, why start a book on learning with stress management? What is stress and what does stress have to do with school?

◆ + + + + + + + + ◆

## What is stress?
## &
## What does it have to do with *school*?

◆ + + + + + + + ◆

It is actually quite simple—stress generally has negative affects on your grades. Based on our experience and research, **stress is the #1 reason for poor academic performance**; grades are not just a reflection of your academic ability. With the help of the Guaranteed A+ PLUS Learning System, we have seen students of all ages and academic backgrounds make dramatic and sustained improvements in their grades!

Here is the truth: we all have brains and all of our brains have the potential to learn. Therefore, if some students are not successful, it is to be concluded then that there must be other factors involved. Most students who do not achieve academic success simply have not found an effective way to manage stress and to master the "job" called studying. Stress often keeps us from performing at our optimal capacity. That is the reason we start with stress management in the Guaranteed A+ PLUS Learning System. After sharing how to manage stress, I will show you how to master the "job of studying."

To manage stress effectively, we first have to understand the nature of stress. **We define stress as anything that takes you away from the task at hand**. In order to make straight A's, you need 100% of your focus on your studies <u>when</u> you are studying. When you have stress in your life, it is very difficult to give 100% of your attention and energy to schoolwork.

❖ ❖ ❖ ❖ ❖ ❖ ❖ ❖ ❖ ❖

## <u>STRESS</u> = Anything that takes you away from the task at hand.

❖ ❖ ❖ ❖ ❖ ❖ ❖ ❖ ❖

## Is Stress Normal?

In the past, when teaching the A+ PLUS Plan, I started each seminar with a stress test that was developed by famous psychologists and psychiatrists. The test is comprised of questions such as: "Do you ever have more to do than seemingly you have time to do?" According to the experts, if you answered "yes" to 4 or more questions out of 13, you are under a significant amount of stress!

It is almost impossible for anyone *not* to answer "yes" to at least a few of the questions on the test, so in the 200+ times I have administered the stress test, everyone failed! The results were so predictable; I stopped giving the test. In short, everyone is under some level of stress.

The point we are trying to make is simple: **Stress is a normal part of everyone's everyday life!** To manage stress the A+ Plus way, we have to change the way we define stress. Generally, when we think of stress we often associate it with major or tragic events that impact our lives, such as car accidents or the death of a family member. While these are legitimate stressors, stress can also come from the "little" pressures that we encounter in our everyday life that bombard our minds. The truth of the matter is that everyone experiences some type of stress daily. As we often say in seminars: instead, life is happening around us every day, and it will continue to happen.

❖ ❖ ❖ ❖ ❖ ❖ ❖ ❖ ❖

## STRESS is NORMAL!

❖ ❖ ❖ ❖ ❖ ❖ ❖ ❖ ❖

Follow the logic here. If stress can "mess with" your grades, it in term can "mess with" your money. Obviously, we don't want that to happen! So we have to find a way to deal with stress. In many of our seminars throughout the years, numerous students have thought of creative ways to eliminate stress forever. Here are some of the examples they have come up with: They would boldly declare—(Perhaps, this might sound familiar to you.) *"This weekend…I am going to get caught up!"* You make a long to-do list and check things off as they are completed. You feel pretty good about yourself in this process. However, a week later, you become depressed when you realize more things have been added to your "to-do" list! The whole process comes to a screeching halt, until a month later you pick up the cycle again and declare: "this weekend…"

Hey, and what about the other line that you sometimes say to yourself: *"Next semester, everything is going to be O.K.!"* Would stress really disappear and your grades magically improve when nothing else in your life has changed? You want different results; yet you haven't done anything differently to make them happen. (I think that is the definition of INSANITY!)

Let's be honest with ourselves. These statements are truly counter-productive because they do not offer real solutions. In reality, statements such as these can actually increase your stress and hurt your grades in the long run. So, our first task in the A+ PLUS Plan is to help people to understand how to manage stress within their lives.

### Famous last words

- *"This weekend…I am going to get caught up!"*

- *"Next semester, everything is going to be O.K.!"*

## How can I manage stress?

**Let's learn how to manage stress, instead of letting it manage you.** The Guaranteed A+ PLUS way to manage stress is surprisingly simple. You will be challenged to develop a stress relieving and preventing activity that only takes 1 to 2 hours weekly by yourself.

✦ ✦ ✦ ✦ ✦ ✦ ✦ ✦ ✦ ✦

### Stress Relieving & Preventing Activity

**1-2 hours per week
By yourself
Both stress relieving & stress preventing**

✦ ✦ ✦ ✦ ✦ ✦ ✦ ✦ ✦ ✦

I will explain this concept through a personal example. There are three things that really relax me: water, reading the Amplified Bible, and prayer. I absolutely love the sound of flowing water. Even when I look at a large body of water (i.e. lake or ocean), it stirs an indescribable sense of peace within my soul. I also love the Amplified Bible because this translation is written in Modern English (no thee's or thou's). It also uses more words to explain the original Greek and Hebrew text. Basically, I understand it more, which inadvertently causes me to enjoy reading it. I also love to pray. Prayer helps me to realize that God is bigger than I can ever imagine and that my problems and concerns are small in comparison. For me, that makes it all good. **How do I combine these 3 things into an activity that I can do for 1 to 2 hours a week by myself?** Students from around the country have come up with some really creative and interesting answers to this question.

- Pray and read my Bible while getting baptized.

- Swim on my back while reading my Bible and pray that my Bible does not get wet. (An engineering student actually designed a gadget for this purpose.)

- Pray while scuba diving, and reading a waterproof Bible.

- Skydive into a lake and pray and recite Bible verses on my way down! (I hope I will never have to do this!)

As creative as they are, these suggestions are not long-term solutions to my stress-management needs. Actually, my stress-management activity is quite simple. A couple of times a week, I take a long hot bubble bath. (I know what you may be thinking...I take showers on other days!) At least once a week, I sit in my extra-deep, extra-long Jacuzzi tub with lots of bubbles, lean my head back on my bath pillow, and pray and read the Bible! This completely relaxes me!

But, my ultimate weekly activity is to pray in the whirlpool. I have a wonderful deal with my health club—they let me stay in the pool area 30 minutes after it closes. When everyone else leaves the water area, I get in the industrial-sized whirlpool and pray. When I get out of the whirlpool, all of the cares and concerns that I had are rolled down the drain with the water droplets. I don't look back and literally I become stress free. For me, this is the ultimate stress relieving and preventing activity.

This Guaranteed A+ PLUS Stress Relieving/Preventing method works because it relieves stress while you are participating in the activity. It also prevents stress because the mere thought of the activity can be relaxing for you. **Your stress relieving/prevention activity should be completely customized to meet your needs.** Here are some examples we have collected from various students.

- Praying while jogging

- Shooting hoops alone

- Drawing or sketching

- Reading a good book

- Playing guitar

As you can see from the examples, it is really easy to find something you can do. One important note: all stress-management activities should be done by yourself. Your ability to relax should not be dependent on others. **The key here is consistent quality time by yourself!**

## *Activity + Motion = Stress Relief / Prevention*

What do you do when you are taking an test and unable to think of the answer to a question that you know you have studied; your frustration and stress levels are increasing because time is ticking; your body tenses up, your heart beats faster and your blood pressure rises—but your stress relieving / preventing activity is playing the guitar (an inappropriate activity in the exam room)?

In situations were you are unable to use your stress relieving / preventing activity to calm down, you need a motion that is related to the activity. The motion's purpose is to remind you of the peace, calm and joyous feelings you had when you were actually doing your activity. With a motion, it is easier to reduce your stress level during situations where you may not be able to do the actual activity.

Since you can't use the guitar during the test, you can use a small motion of playing air guitar. Simply lean back a little, take a deep breath and play your favorite cord or song, imagining you are actually playing your guitar. Believe it or not, this allows you to unplug a bit from the current stress, reduce your mental stress level and allow your body to relax and your mind to think clearly. Don't be surprised if the answer to the question suddenly pops into your head.

Your motion doesn't need to be a gigantic motion to get the job done, just something to remind yourself how wonderful you felt the last time you engaged in your stress relieving / preventing activity.

# Chapter I Review

We have covered three major points in Chapter I.

1. **Stress: Anything that takes you away from the task at hand**

2. **Stress = Normal**

3. **Stress Relieving & Preventing Activity**
   - 1-2 hours per week
   - By yourself
   - Both stress relieving & stress preventing!

## *Guaranteed A+ PLUS Exercises*

1. **Write down your own A+ PLUS stress relieving/preventing activity.**

   _____

   _____

2. **Please schedule a weekly time for your activity.**

3. **Design a motion for your stress relieving/preventing activity.**

Example:
- My own stress management activity is to play the guitar.

- I will do this activity every Thursday from 4 – 6 p.m.
  - You can still play the guitar anytime you want.
  - However, Thursday from 4-6 p.m. is now set aside as your "personal time"!

- My motion is "playing an air guitar"!

# Chapter II

✦ ✦ ✦ ✦ ✦ ✦ ✦ ✦ ✦ ✦ ✦ ✦ ✦

# *Time Management*

## WHAT to do vs. HOW to do it

This is the most distinctive characteristic of the Guaranteed A+ PLUS Learning System. There are many study skills programs that will tell you **WHAT to do** as well as give you plenty of good advice. But we have found that going a step further will make your studying easier. Within this chapter, we are going to show you **HOW to do it and how to do it in a more efficient way**. Instead of just telling you not to procrastinate (like you have heard a thousand times before); we will share practical step-by-step methods about how to manage your time.

✦ ✦ ✦ ✦ ✦ ✦ ✦ ✦ ✦

**You may have heard:**
Make sure you manage your time
& don't procrastinate!

**Guaranteed A+ PLUS says:**
Let us show you how to PLAN for success
step-by-step!

✦ ✦ ✦ ✦ ✦ ✦ ✦ ✦ ✦

As a high school student, your schedule is relatively routine. You go to school in the morning and attend a set number of classes from Monday through Friday. You may participate in some extra-curricular activities such as sports, clubs or volunteering after school. Also, you probably hang out with friends, watch TV, play video games, etc. or you might have to work. If it is a good day, you may even do some homework before dinner!

> What do high school students do with their time every week?

There are exactly 168 hours in every week. (It is true...you can do the math!) For many students, it sounds like a lot of hours. But that is because **we generally don't think about time from the perspective of a full week.**

Let's get started by looking at how a **typical high school student who is _not_ on the A+ PLUS Plan spends his or her time.** We will fill out the table below by using some numbers based on documented national averages and basic common sense.

Don't worry if your situation is different. In Part 2, Y.C. will take you through a step-by-step procedure to create your own individual schedule.

## *What You Do In A Week*

| Activity | National Average (Hours/Week) |
|---|---|
| Sleep | |
| Eat | |
| Social | |
| Class | |
| Study | |
| Personal Hygiene (PH) | |
| Relax / Planning | |
| Church / Worship | |
| Work | |
| Extra-curricular Activities | |
| Exercise | |
| Laundry / Cleaning | |
| Errands | |
| Transportation | |
| **Total** | |

## *SLEEP*

Who does not want to sleep 8 hours a day? In fact, the **Guaranteed A+ PLUS Plan guarantees you up to 8 hours of sleep a night**. Yes, you can get 8 hours of sleep a night *and* still make all A's. WAIT...I can prove that this is possible. Here is my personal testimony: my freshman year in college, I went to bed at 10:00 p.m. every night. (Don't worry; you don't have to go to bed by 10:00 p.m. to be on the

A+ PLUS Plan.) I have since discovered my natural bedtime is probably around 2:00 a.m. – 4:00 a.m. One of the benefits of owning your own company is the ability to set your own schedule: my office opens at noon!

When I was growing up, my mother set my bedtime to be 10:00 p.m. on school nights. Of course, as a child, I tested the limit of my bedtime curfew by staying up past this time to watch TV. My mother's discipline is what I call "old-school." My definition of "old school" is that your parents communicated both verbally and physically—smile if you can relate. While her physical communication was never abusive, it was certainly effective! When my mother found me up past my bedtime, she would "communicate" with me! After a couple of those "physical communication sessions," my body became trained. So, even after I went away to college, my body shut down automatically at 10:00 p.m. to avoid pain. I am living proof that you can sleep 8 hours per night, get all A's and still be a normal high school student involved in many extra-curricular activities with a great social life.

## EAT

Generally, students spend about 15 minutes per day for breakfast, 45 minutes for lunch, an hour for dinner and 30 minutes for various snacking. That comes out to be 2.5 hours per day and rounds up to be 18 hours a week!

## SOCIAL

This is a very popular item on the schedule. The social entity includes hanging out with friends, watching TV, reading emails, instant messaging, talking on the telephone, movies and visiting with family members. We're going to estimate the time to be 21 hours per week or 3 hours a day.

## CLASS

The average high school student spends about 30 hours in class every week.

## STUDY

If a student is on the college-prep track and preparing to go to a competitive 4-year university, he or she will spend 22.5 hours a week studying as a 10-11$^{th}$ grader in high school. That is more than 3 hours a day – 7 days a week. (Don't get scared. We will come back to talk about this number.)

## PERSONAL HYGIENE

Here is a non-negotiable activity! You get 1 hour a day for personal hygiene whether you think you need it or not! That is at least 7 hours per week. (Please utilize this time wisely to avoid creating any issues for your friends…SMILE!)

## RELAX

This is absolutely critical and it is part of the stress management activity. We estimate an hour per day for your relaxation time and an extra hour for the big weekly activity. This is a total of 8 hours.

## CHURCH/WORSHIP

This estimate varies greatly. The average number given by students in our seminars is generally about 3 hours per week.

## WORK

Let's assume this student works 10 hours per week.

## EXTRA-CURRICULAR

Typical high school students spend about 3-7 hours per week participating in extra-curricular activities, such as clubs, sports, volunteering, etc. Let's use an average of 5 hours per week. Of course, this number varies greatly from person to person.

## EXERCISE

Let's assume you can get 3 hours of aerobic exercise in each week. (Of course, the assumption behind the assumption is that you are currently exercising.)

## LAUNDRY/CLEANING

We generally schedule 2 hours for both laundry and cleaning. Laundry is one of the activities that you can multi-task. (There is really no point to sitting and watching the spin cycle!)

As far as cleaning goes, we are about to make your parents really happy! As part of the Guaranteed A+ PLUS Plan, **you are going to keep your room clean, everyday**! It is extremely difficult to function in an orderly fashion when there is disorder around you. A clean and orderly room will greatly help you improve your productivity!

Don't worry! This is a full-service book. We can even show you how to keep your room in order. Most of the time, there are 3 reasons your room is dirty or disorderly.

1. Piles of paper or books

2. Piles of clothes

3. Bed unmade!

In Part 2 of this book, we will show you how to make your bed in 3 seconds or less and other short cuts that are guaranteed to keep your room clean! (Please refer to FAQ #15 & 16 in Part 2 of this book.)

## ERRANDS

Let's throw in 2 hours a week for errands. You may have to go to the mall or video store periodically!

## TRANSPORTATION

Since time to walk between classes is included in the school hour, transportation here refers to getting to/from school and other places. So, we will budget 5 hours for transportation.

Now, we have finished outlining the weekly tasks and their estimated times. Let's take a look at the bigger picture.

## What You Do in A Week

| Activity | Students NOT on Plan (Hours/Week) |
|---|---|
| Sleep | 56 |
| Eat | 18 |
| Social | 21 |
| Class | 30 |
| Study | 22.5 |
| Personal Hygiene (PH) | 7 |
| Relax / Planning | 8 |
| Church / Worship | 3 |
| Work | 10 |
| Extra-curricular Activities | 5 |
| Exercise | 3 |
| Laundry / Cleaning | 2 |
| Errands | 2 |
| Transportation | 5 |
| **Total** | **192.5 hours / week** |

**Wow, an average student NOT on the A+ PLUS Plan needs 192.5 hours per week**. That is *24.5 hours* that we don't have. We need an extra day and 30 minutes just to do all the things we need to do!

Remember the question on the stress test from Chapter 1: "Do you ever have more to do than you have time to do it in?"

✦ ✦ ✦ ✦ ✦ ✦ ✦ ✦ ✦ ✦

## Extra 24.5 Hours Needed = STRESS!

✦ ✦ ✦ ✦ ✦ ✦ ✦ ✦ ✦ ✦

**Don't get discouraged!** Guaranteed 4.0 offers a way out! We are going to review the time analysis and label all of the non-negotiable items with a **star** in the left column. **Non-negotiable means the activity must be done and it must be done at a particular time.**

### SLEEP

**Definitely a non-negotiable activity**! You don't want to get or stay on the cycle of mediocrity. The *cycle of mediocrity* is defined by the following characteristics:

- You fall asleep and miss important information in class. You have to stay up late trying to understand what you missed in class from the book and then attempt to do homework. And though you didn't finish the homework, you did turn it in before falling asleep in class again. After all, you are too tired to pay attention anyway.

- The cycle continues. You have a chemistry test coming up—so, you drop everything and cram for chemistry. You take the exam and think you passed. Now an English paper is due. Drop everything to write the paper and turn it in at the last minute. Oh no, then you notice that your math homework is due tomorrow and you haven't even started on it. On top of that, your history group project meeting is tomorrow too and you have not finished your part! Now you wonder if you should do the homework or prep for the group meeting.

**The cycle of mediocrity starts with inadequate sleep which takes you into a downward spiral**. You are continually tired, worn down and stressed. You still only make average or below average grades. We call this unnecessary drama. Fortunately, on the A+ PLUS Plan, sleep is non-negotiable and guaranteed!

### EAT

Honestly, you don't really put fork to mouth for 18 hours a week. (If you did, you would be a lot bigger!) Most of the time, we eat with friends or family, and mix socializing with eating. More often than not, we sit at the lunch table with the "coulda, shoulda and woulda" conversation. "I woulda studied but…I coulda made a better grade if…I should be studying now except I am sitting here talking to you." If we separate the social time from the eating time, we can easily reduce this number to 8 hours per week.

✦ ✦ ✦ ✦ ✦ ✦ ✦ ✦ ✦ ✦

## *Guaranteed A+ PLUS Time Management Principle #1*
## Whatever you do, do it 100%!

✦ ✦ ✦ ✦ ✦ ✦ ✦ ✦ ✦ ✦

The principle here is to fully utilize your time. When it's time to socialize, enjoy your friends 100%. If you are eating with friends, have fun. Don't sit around having "coulda, shoulda, or woulda" conversations. When it is time to study, give studying 100% of your attention.

### CLASS

Non-negotiable! If you want to get an A+ PLUS, you simply must go to class!

### STUDY

If you want an A+ PLUS using our brain-based learning strategies, **study time is absolutely…negotiable!** Here is the secret to the balanced life of an A+ PLUS student: Guaranteed A+ PLUS can cut your study time from 22.5 hours to about 11 hours. **By increasing your efficiency and effectiveness, we can reduce your study time by almost 50%.** The Guaranteed 3 steps in chapter 3 will show you how to accomplish this in detail.

Please note: once you decide to follow the A+ PLUS Plan and cut study time in half, study time becomes **NON-NEGOTIABLE!**

✦ ✦ ✦ ✦ ✦ ✦ ✦ ✦ ✦ ✦

## *Guaranteed A+ PLUS Time Management Principle #2*
## ON PLAN - Reduce study time!

✦ ✦ ✦ ✦ ✦ ✦ ✦ ✦ ✦ ✦

### RELAX

That's right, non-negotiable! No one is a robot and if you refuse to relax, your body will likely take a break for you—possibly in the form of sickness.

### PERSONAL HYGIENE

Yes, non-negotiable! Stay civilized!

## CHURCH/WORSHIP

For people who go to church or practice worship traditions, this is really a non-negotiable activity. It is hard to call up your pastor or priest and ask them to reschedule service because you are going to be busy Sunday morning. It probably won't go over too well.

Let's look at the time analysis table one more time. With the changes in **EAT** and **STUDY** alone we have reduced the schedule by 21.4 hours and we are now only 3 hours away from 168! The number can easily be made up from either extra-curricular involvement or work, depending on your personal schedule!

### What You Do In A Week

| | Activity | ON PLAN AVERAGE (Hours/Week) |
|---|---|---|
| ✸ | Sleep | 56 |
| | Eat | 8 |
| | Social | 21 |
| ✸ | Class | 30 |
| ✸ | Study | 11 |
| ✸ | Personal Hygiene (PH) | 7 |
| ✸ | Relax / Planning | 8 |
| ( ✸ ) | Church / Worship | 3 |
| | Work | 10 |
| | Extra-curricular Activities | 5 |
| | Exercise | 3 |
| ✸ | Laundry / Cleaning | 2 |
| | Errands | 2 |
| | Transportation | 5 |
| | **Total** | **171** |

Since everyone's schedule is different, we won't spend time to "nickel and dime" this hypothetical schedule. Again, in Part 2, Y.C. will take you through a simple way to create your perfect schedule.

Did you notice something interesting? What is the combined total of class and study time? It is 30+11 = 41 hours per week!

## 30 + 11 = 41 HOURS PER WEEK

Wait a minute; what does 41 hours a week sound like? A full-time JOB and a bit extra! Please work with me, I want the lightbulb to go on! School is really your job.

✦ ✦ ✦ ✦ ✦ ✦ ✦ ✦ ✦ ✦

## *Guaranteed A+ PLUS Time Management Principle #3*
## School = My JOB!

✦ ✦ ✦ ✦ ✦ ✦ ✦ ✦ ✦ ✦

This may seem like a new revelation for you as a student. **School was your job ever since you became a student; you just never really thought of it that way!** Even when you go to college, school is still your job.

A college student can spend at least 15 hours in class and 45 hours studying every week. This is NOT an exaggeration! The Guaranteed A+ PLUS plan can reduce these college study hours by almost half as well to 25 hours. However, it still adds up to 40 hours! (15 + 25 = 40 hours.) **Bottom line, School really is your job!**

| | Activity | Time Estimates (Hours/ Week) | Time Estimates (Hours/ Week) |
|---|---|---|---|
| | | Without A+ PLUS Plan | With A+ PLUS Plan |
| ✹ | Class (High School) | 30 | 30 |
| ✹ | Study | ~~22.5~~ | 11 |

| | Activity | Time Estimates (Hours/ Week) | Time Estimates (Hours/ Week) |
|---|---|---|---|
| | | Without the Guaranteed 4.0 Plan | On the Guaranteed 4.0 Plan |
| ✹ | Class (College) | 15 | 15 |
| ✹ | Study | ~~45~~ | 25 |

**REALITY CHECK: School is MY JOB**

If we were to be honest, then we need to ask ourselves this question: "Am I studying as hard as a full-time working person?" Also, let's look at the flip side of the coin. When people come home from work, they generally don't take work home with them. This same principle should apply to school. If we take care of school business **by following the A+ PLUS Plan, we can have a 40-hour week schedule with little or no studying on weekends**!

*Are you working two JOBS?*

If school is your full-time job, what is this activity on the list called "work"? It is, in fact, a second job! Having two jobs normally presents some complications.

If school is your full-time job; then I want you to do it well. Generally, people get rewarded based on how well they do their job. And high school and college are not any different. Good grades in high school and college are rewarded with college scholarships, internship and job opportunities, and higher salaries. I strongly suggest making an investment in your future by staying "On Plan" now and reaping big time later.

Please note that "WORK" **is NOT** labeled as a non-negotiable activity. On the A+ PLUS plan, it is ok for high school students to work. However, there are some basic guidelines we want you to follow if you want to work. If you are looking for a job while you are in high school, here is the scoop.

❖ ❖ ❖ ❖ ❖ ❖ ❖ ❖ ❖

## Pick a job that will:

- **Help you now: real-life exposure**
- **Help you later: college application**
- **Reduce time away from studying (i.e. minimal travel time)**

❖ ❖ ❖ ❖ ❖ ❖ ❖ ❖ ❖

"Help you now" means finding a job that can help you gain some real-life exposure and responsibilities. To "help you later" is to find a job that will look good and support your college application. "Reduce time away from studying" is simple; find a job that has a flexible schedule that won't hinder your effort to be on the A+ PLUS Plan.

For example, if you are interested in majoring in business, stocking groceries at the store is not as good a job as working as an office intern with a local merchant. While both will give you some real-life exposure, an office intern position will help you learn more about the world of business. An office job in your field is much more impressive on your college application.

Here are some trade-offs for high school students and their parents to consider when it comes to work.

## Working vs. Playing Sports

If you are heavily involved in sports, working during the season may not be a good idea. A typical high school sport, such as basketball or tennis, can take up to

10-15 hours per week between practices, games and transportation time. Adding the physical demands on your body to the equation, it will be difficult to concentrate on school if you are playing a sport and working at the same time.

## Working during school year vs. summer

Some students only want to work during summer when traditionally seasonal jobs are plentiful. There are no hard and fast rules on this one. However, please keep in mind that summer is also prime time for extra-curricular activities such as visiting college campuses, participating in pre-college programs, conferences or taking advantage of study abroad opportunities.

## Working vs. Volunteering

With careful investigation, you will discover many internship programs or research opportunities available for majors you may be interested in. Some only take place during the summer, but some are yearlong opportunities. While high school students generally do not receive a paycheck for their work, involvement in these programs gives students a tremendous advantage on their college application as well as career planning.

If you did not find a structured program that is suitable for your situation, you can consider creating your own. For example, if you are interested in veterinary medicine, you may approach your local vet and ask if they would mentor you, and ask about the possibility of volunteering in their office. You can structure it as a semester-long commitment so you can get your feet wet in the field. With some creativity and persistence, you can make it work for you.

❖ ❖ ❖ ❖ ❖ ❖ ❖ ❖ ❖ ❖

### Major trade-offs to be considered about work for a high school student

- **Working vs. Playing Sports**
- **Working during school year vs. Summer**
- **Working vs. Volunteering**

❖ ❖ ❖ ❖ ❖ ❖ ❖ ❖ ❖ ❖

By the way, we **don't recommend that high school freshmen or college freshmen work at all!** The transition into high school and from high school to college can be difficult—academically and personally. You may not want to complicate it by overtaxing yourself with work.

Now we have covered all the bases. Let's move on to the rest of the Guaranteed A+ PLUS Plan!

# Chapter II Review

- There are only 168 hours per week.

- Students NOT on The Guaranteed A+ PLUS Plan
  - Need at least 192.5 hours per week
  - Extra 24.5 hours needed = Stress

- Guaranteed A+ PLUS Time Management Principles
  - Whatever you do, do it 100%!
  - On A+ PLUS Plan - Reduce study time!
  - School is my JOB!
    - Class + Study > 40 hours per week!

- Pick a job that will:
  - Help you now: real-life exposure
  - Help you later: college application
  - Reduce time away from studying
    (i.e. minimal travel time)

- Major trade-offs to be considered about work for a high school student
  - Working vs. Playing Sports
  - Working during school year vs. Summer
  - Working vs. Volunteering

# Chapter III

+ + + + ◆ ◆ ◆ ◆ + + +

# *Guaranteed 3 Steps to A+ PLUS*

## Step 1: Unwritten Rules of the Classroom

In this section, we will focus on the foundations of the Guaranteed A+ PLUS Learning System. Buckle up and let's get started! **Step one is highly technical**. In fact, I want 100% of your attention focused on getting it down exactly…. Step 1: GO TO CLASS!

Yes, you read that correctly, GO TO CLASS. You may be wondering why I would waste time to point out such a simple fact; after all, we all claim to understand the importance of attending classes. Yet, the effect of this simple step is often underestimated. In this section, I will show you some of the secret unwritten rules of the classroom beyond simple class attendance.

Class attendance is one of the most foundational, yet most ignored rules in school. On average, about 100 students attend a Guaranteed A+ PLUS seminar. When I get to this point, I often issue a challenge to these students: "If you know how to cut a class and not get caught (not saying that you have done it but maybe your friends have), please raise your hand." And guess what? Practically everyone's hand will go up in the air, some very quickly. I've seen seminars where **every hand is raised along with some incriminating laughter.** And it does not pay to lie in this demonstration because friends of the offenders (who know the painful truth) generally raise the hand of the lying student for them; giving new meaning to the term "public embarrassment"!

◆ ◆ ◆ ◆ ◆ ◆ ◆ ◆ ◆ ◆

## Step 1: GO TO CLASS

◆ ◆ ◆ ◆ ◆ ◆ ◆ ◆ ◆ ◆

This demonstration gets my point across: **d**espite all of the attendance-taking measures and being required to go to school by law, many students still **treat class as an optional activity!** My experience is that we make bad decisions when we forget the benefits we can receive from being in class! Let's take a moment to remind ourselves of what we know so well already.

Let's talk about money once more. At first glance, high school seems to be "FREE" if you attend a public school. However, the old adage is true: "There is no such thing as free lunch." What you may perceive is a "free" education actually costs a big chunk of tax money from your parents. In fact, in the most recent data available (year 2002-03), the United States spent $388 billion dollars on all students in public elementary, middle, and high schools. It may be hard to imagine such a big number as 388,000,000,000 dollars and see what it really means. There are 48.2 million students in the United States. So, if we do the math, the average cost of one year of your public education in high school is approximately $8049.79. In hourly terms, you end up paying $7-8 per hour of class.

> **The average cost of one day of your high school experience is about $50.**

## Visualize this:

I am taking out a brand new $100 bill from my wallet. I am taking the bill out slowly and carefully so it stays new and crisp. To your surprise, I am placing the $100 in your hand and saying: "Keep it!" To be certain this is not a practical joke, you put the money up to the lightbulb to make sure it is real. You see the embedded strip next to Ben Franklin's face. You start to get excited because the money is real! Then I snatch the $100 from you, crumble it up, tear it in half and toss it into a nearby fireplace! You can only watch hopelessly as the $100 bill turns into a pile of ashes. Are your feelings hurt, yet? You wanted to keep that $100, didn't you?

You may think: "I would never throw money away like that!" Guess again! **Every time you miss school, you are literally throwing money away!** Each missed day of school costs you at least $50. Maybe in the course of 3 weeks you managed to miss 2 days of school. Congratulations! You have just thrown away $100.

The story does not end there. Once you finish high school, a college education will easily cost you or your family a small fortune. Here is the national average on how much you would pay for 1 hour of lecture in college.

| Type of Institution | Average Cost of 1 hour of Lecture |
|---|---|
| Public High School | $7 - 8 per hour |
| 2-year Community College | $5 - 10 per hour |
| 4-year Public University | $15 - 50 per hour |
| 4-year Private University | $50 - 125 per hour |

If you are missing school now and throwing money away now when teachers are taking class attendance, how will you make sure that you are not burning money once you are in college?

✦ ✦ ✦ ✦ ✦ ✦ ✦ ✦ ✦ ✦

## *Why should you go to class?*
## Reason #1: Because YOU paid for it!

✦ ✦ ✦ ✦ ✦ ✦ ✦ ✦ ✦ ✦

Let's say that you graduated from college and got a wonderful job with a great company. After receiving your big "sign on" bonus, you pick out your dream car. It is loaded with the leather package, state-of-the-art sound system and alloy wheels: the works. Then, you sign on the dotted line and become the proud owner of your new "wheels." Now, let me ask you this question: Would you leave your new car and take the bus home? Of course not! **You wouldn't because you paid for it! Be honest, you wouldn't even go to McDonald's and order a Happy Meal and NOT get your toy!**

School is the only place where people pay full price for something and they are happy when they DO NOT get the goods. **Unlike other purchases, there are no refunds from school when you miss class!** Missing class is exactly the same as purposely throwing a $100 bill into the fire. So, you are not stupid, you are not going to throw money away by missing classes. Please say out loud: "I am not stupid; I will not throw money away, I will go to class, every class, every day!"

**How about another extra million on top of the $ 1.5 million?**

$100 may seem like a lot of money (especially to high school students), but your education is worth a lot more than $100 in the long run. How about $10,000? Consider two high school students that went to the same college and had the same major. Student A has learned the secret rules of the classroom and earned almost straight A's in college. Student B just barely got by with a C average in college. Following graduation, they went to work for the same company. The difference in their starting salaries is at least $10,000 a year!

This is only the beginning. If we calculated the salary difference over the course of an average career, the extra $10,000 grows to a mind-boggling extra $1,000,000 for student A! That is an extra million dollars on top of the 1.5 million dollars we discussed in the introduction! Just remember the $2.5 million dollars the next time a "friend" wants you to cut class with him.

✦ ✦ ✦ ✦ ✦ ✦ ✦ ✦ ✦

## *Why should you go to class?*

## Reason #2: There is critical information communicated in class that you need!

✦ ✦ ✦ ✦ ✦ ✦ ✦ ✦ ✦

Sometimes it is easy to just "BE" in class physically while our minds are as far away as China, and more interested in what will happen during lunch period. It is simply not enough to be in class physically, we should go to class and pay attention because **we will receive important information** that often makes life, *oh* so much easier.

Allow me to share a real-life horror story. (Names have been changed to protect the guilty!) Mike was in a math class but was temporarily distracted by his friends' conversation. There was a test scheduled for Friday. However, when Mike and his friends were chuckling about the movie they saw the prior weekend, they ALL missed a very important announcement. The teacher had moved the test a day early. Needless to say, they were shocked when they came to class on Thursday because they were surprised by the test! We call this type of experience unnecessary drama! Unfortunately, these unnecessary dramas repeat themselves often in high school. For example, a student who cuts class or was not paying attention may miss the following:

- A teacher changes the due date for assignments

- A major hint for the next test

- A pop quiz given at the end of class

- Extra-credit assignments

My strong recommendation: save yourself some stress and go to class! Be there physically and mentally!

✦ ✦ ✦ ✦ ✦ ✦ ✦ ✦ ✦

## *Why should you go to class?*
## Reason #3: To Learn!

✦ ✦ ✦ ✦ ✦ ✦ ✦ ✦ ✦

Yes, we know we are definitely overstating the obvious, but you do go to class to learn! Sometimes it can be difficult to focus on your academics when there are extra-curricular activities, friends, and numerous social events, all demanding your time and competing for your attention. The idea is to handle your business and learn the material during class so you can chill when you are out of class, instead of worrying about school.

And by the way, you want to be in class on time with paper and pen ready to go! Have you ever started to pull out your notebook at the moment the teacher started speaking? It takes a while to catch up, pay attention to the on-going lecture and try to take notes all at the same time, doesn't it? It can take 5 minutes to get adjusted and up to date and that is 5 minutes worth of "possible test material" that you just missed. Don't worry; you can still chat with your friends before class starts. All I ask is that you take out your paper and pen before the teacher starts speaking!

Now that we are all set to attend class, let's talk about where we should sit. **You should sit front and center**! "But…I want to sit in the back!" said one student. If someone lets you choose your own seat in your favorite music group's concert or a sporting event, would you choose the back row in the nosebleed section? No! I don't think so. You probably would fight to get as close to the front as possible just in case you might get a free backstage pass!

✦ ✦ ✦ ✦ ✦ ✦ ✦ ✦ ✦

## *Where should I sit in class?*
## Front & Center

✦ ✦ ✦ ✦ ✦ ✦ ✦ ✦ ✦

The same principle applies here; you'll want the best seat your money can buy. In this case, **the best seats in the classroom are located front and center.** Front and center puts you in the best position to learn. These seats are known as the "Learning T." Statistically, students sitting in the front and center make A's in the class! What is so magical about these seats?

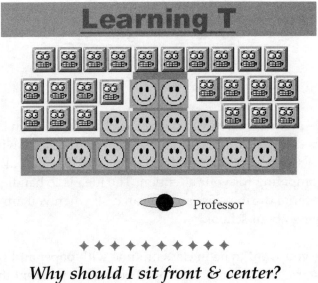

Professor

✦ ✦ ✦ ✦ ✦ ✦ ✦ ✦ ✦ ✦

### *Why should I sit front & center?*
### Fewer Distractions

✦ ✦ ✦ ✦ ✦ ✦ ✦ ✦ ✦ ✦

The first reason for you to sit front and center is: **there are fewer distractions!** Imagine being late for a movie or church service. You would probably tiptoe in the door and sit in the back to avoid drawing undue attention. You can end up being distracted throughout the event. Instead of enjoying the movie peacefully, you constantly notice all the people who are in front of you, especially if they are talking, kissing or tall enough to obstruct your view. Or, instead of focusing on the church service, you wonder about why Mr. Lee's hair looks like a toupee and why Mrs. Murphy wears that funny-looking hat! I am sure you have been distracted in this way because we all have!

Our brains are very complex and process tremendous amounts of information about our surroundings every single second. When triggered by memory, sight, sound or other conditions, our brains will generate thoughts that may not be related to the task at hand. Therefore, we are distracted. In other words, **we have enough of our own internal distractions; we don't need help from anyone else.** (Ever wonder what you are thinking about when you are not thinking about anything in particular?)

An expert said in an average classroom of students:

- 10% are interested

- 10% have no clue or interest

- 80% are engaged in daydreaming, fantasy or distracted by their surroundings

Now, keep it real for a moment. If you can get distracted while watching your favorite TV show or music video, you can easily become very distracted during a class that does not excite you; especially if you are in a warm classroom after eating a big lunch. By sitting front and center, you reduce external sources of distraction to a minimum. This allows you to focus on the class material!

✦ ✦ ✦ ✦ ✦ ✦ ✦ ✦ ✦ ✦

## *Why should you sit front & center?*
## First Impressions

✦ ✦ ✦ ✦ ✦ ✦ ✦ ✦ ✦ ✦

Now here is one more of those unwritten rules you have been waiting for! **Make sure you sit in the front row on the first day of class.** This should not be hard to do—the first row tends to be very empty on the first day. Please note: On day one, your teacher will scan the faces of students in the front row. Automatically, they will assume these are "A" students. Why? Their assumption is based on years of experience. The majority of their former "A" students sat front and center. To most of them, it may be a subconscious thought. But, behold the **power of first impressions!**

We know that first impressions are hard to overcome. So, ask yourself: "If my teacher is going to have a first impression of me, should it be that I am an 'A' student or just an average student?" A **positive first impression has great benefits for you.** When your teacher thinks that you are an "A" student, they will treat you like one! Teachers generally help students that they perceive to be "A" students more than others. This could mean more eye contact with you during lectures to make sure that you understand the material. They are often more willing to offer help if you are having difficulties. They may even give some insight that will come in handy when prepping for exams.

✦ ✦ ✦ ✦ ✦ ✦ ✦ ✦ ✦

## *Why should I sit front & Center?*
## 1. Fewer Distractions
## 2. First Impressions

✦ ✦ ✦ ✦ ✦ ✦ ✦ ✦ ✦

Allow me to give you a personal example. I have worn glasses since I was 6 years old. I sat front and center all my life just trying to see. (Thank God for thin-lens technology and cool, funky frames.) So, there I was, a freshman enrolled in an English class at the University of Texas. On the first day, my teacher saw me sitting front and center and assumed I was an "A" student. The first paper I wrote, he gave me an A+!

Now the story takes an interesting turn! Have you ever read something that you did not quite understand and yet you had to write about it? That was my situation with the second paper. I was stuck for days and did not know how to write the essay. It was 11:30 the night before the paper was due and I thought I was going to die. (Remember the story from time management? I had been trained to fall out at 10 p.m.!) In my moment of desperation, I started writing down random sentences and incomplete thoughts. At this point, I didn't care anymore. I just wanted the assignment to be over. When I got to 500 words, I said, "That is all I can do!" I went to bed. When I turned the essay in the next day, I simply did not care!

However, the day I was supposed to get the paper back, I started to care again! I began to worry because that term paper was worth 1/4 of my grade. During the long walk to class, I calculated worst-case scenarios: "Ok, I got an A+ on the first paper. If the teacher showed some mercy, I may have a D on the second one. If I get an A+ on the third paper and do extra credit assignments, maybe I can pull a B out of this class!"

When I finally got my paper back, I could not believe my eyes. I really believe that it hurt the teacher so much not to be able to give me an A, he gave me a B+ instead! Underneath the grade, he wrote, "If you're having any personal problems or difficulties, please feel free to drop by my office." (This shows you how bad the mumble-jumble essay really was.)

**Why did he give me a B+ when I deserved a very different grade?** It is because he perceived me to be an "A" student! Of course, my first A+ paper proved his assumption to be true. As a result, when I failed to produce "A" work on the second paper, the teacher believed that outside factors were negatively impacting my work! In short, I got the benefit of the doubt. Of course, I "handled my business" and wrote an "A" paper for my next assignment. By doing so, I confirmed the teacher's first impression of me as an "A" student.

**Some students ask me: "What do you do if you have assigned seating in a class?"** There is a simple answer to this: ask your teacher nicely if you can be re-seated to the front and center part of the classroom so you can pay more attention in the class. Depending on the situation, sometimes it is better to ask your parents to request a new seat for you. Some teachers would re-seat you right away; some may not be able to change the entire seating chart for you. However, even if they can't change your seat, the teacher will automatically pay more attention to you from that point on because you demonstrated a desire to learn. In short, you created front and center wherever you are sitting in the classroom.

**So, go to class everyday, sit front and center and reap the benefits from these unwritten rules of the classroom.** Now, we can move on to Step 2…

# Step 1 Review: Go to Class!

**Why should I go to class?**
1. I paid for it!
2. Important information is given in class that I need!
3. To learn!

**Where should I sit in class?**
- Front & Center
- Sit in the Learning T!

**Why should I sit front & center?**
1. Fewer Distractions
2. First Impressions

## Guaranteed A+ PLUS Exercise

|  | Name of Class | Am I sitting in the "T-Zone"? (Yes or No) | If not, how can I be re-seated? |
|---|---|---|---|
| Class 1 |  |  |  |
| Class 2 |  |  |  |
| Class 3 |  |  |  |
| Class 4 |  |  |  |
| Class 5 |  |  |  |
| Class 6 |  |  |  |
|  |  |  |  |
|  |  |  |  |

# Step 2: Secrets & Insights about Your Teacher

Here we go. **Step 2: "Go See Your Teacher At Least Once Per Week!"**

Every time we get to this part of the seminar, students ask: "Do I really have to see the teacher?" There is an occasional moan coupled with "I don't feel comfortable talking to all my teachers." Some students seem to equate seeing a teacher outside of class to a trip to the dentist. **We are going to share with you** special insights about your teacher **in this section.** I promise you that this step won't hurt a bit (or at least not as bad as your last dentist appointment).

This information will make it easier to relate to your teacher and get understanding of your class material. Have you ever received second or third-hand information, and then later discovered that it really didn't happen that way at all? (Don't you just hate rumors spreading in school?)

As a result of "he-said, she-said," facts are usually distorted or critical information is missing. When you have a question about a homework problem, do you want a questionable answer from your friends or an absolute correct answer from your teacher? The sensible choice is your teacher. I want you to go straight to the source to get all your questions answered. Quite simply, your teacher has first-hand information.

✦ ✦ ✦ ✦ ✦ ✦ ✦ ✦ ✦

## *Why & When Should I Go See My Teacher?*

- **To get first-hand information**
- **During Teacher's Office Hours (TOH)**

✦ ✦ ✦ ✦ ✦ ✦ ✦ ✦ ✦

### *What is TOH and why should I do it?*

Let's break it down. TOH stands for Teacher's Office Hours. This is a designated time that you can visit your teacher. **For most high school students, it usually means before or after school or a tutorial period, if your school has one.** For all practical purposes, your teacher controls every aspect of the course! There is one person who knows everything you need to know in order to make an A in the class. That person is your teacher. So, who should you see every week?

One of the first things that people ask: "Isn't that just brown-nosing?" My answer is "NO!" **The goal of seeing your teacher is to get proper understanding of the class material.** You should go to TOH to review concepts or ask questions. In addition, you will most likely develop a favorable rapport with faculty members because of your effort to learn. (That is a pretty good by-product.) In addition, once you get to know them, asking them for a college recommendation will be a snap!

Many students ask me: "What if I don't have any questions?" My response is: "GO ANYWAY!" If you are not getting an A in that class already, it means you are missing something somewhere! If you need a starting point, gather your old homework or exams from the class, redo the problems you missed and ask your teacher if you did it right the second time!

Even if you have an A, you should still go. Another reason to go to TOH is to test your understanding by explaining a concept from class to your teacher. Be sure to explain the concept in your own words, so your teacher can point out the possible details you may have missed and share any additional helpful hints and information. During TOH, teachers have more time to explain the homework or lecture. Once you understand the principle in detail, you can tackle related homework or exam problems with ease. Bottom line: this type of understanding is extremely beneficial for your grades.

✦ ✦ ✦ ✦ ✦ ✦ ✦ ✦ ✦ ✦

## *Need a starting point?*

- **Discuss corrected homework/exam problems**
- **Explain a concept to your teacher**

✦ ✦ ✦ ✦ ✦ ✦ ✦ ✦ ✦

## *3 Secrets About Your Professors (that every student should know!)*

While we are in step 2, we are going to share 3 secrets about your teacher that no one will tell you. Truly, most students never figure them out until way too late.

✦ ✦ ✦ ✦ ✦ ✦ ✦ ✦ ✦ ✦

### *3 secrets about your Teachers:* 1. Teachers are people, too!

✦ ✦ ✦ ✦ ✦ ✦ ✦ ✦ ✦ ✦

There is an urban legend that says teachers are aliens who come to earth to do mind experiments on students. I am happy to disprove this myth! Research on teachers all over the country has shown that each of them has a human mother and father! **Yes, they are people!** Wow, this is a discovery worthy of a Nobel Prize! It stands to reason, if teachers are people, it also means that **they have feelings—just like you.**

In truth, many of us do not extend the basic courtesy of considering our teacher's feelings. If you were the teacher, how would you feel if a student repeatedly fell asleep in your class? Just imagine yourself as a teacher for a moment. You look out into the classroom and all you see are students slumping down in their chairs, some yawning and half-asleep, some talking to their friends, and some caring less what you have to say. When the students do participate, they speak to you rudely as if you should pay them to sit in class. How do you feel right now as the teacher? Do you still want to teach this class?

If you are the only student in your class who nods on purpose and pays complete attention to the lecture, your teacher will end up teaching directly to you. Whose grade do you think the teacher will be most interested in? Who can easily go to your teacher for a glowing letter of recommendation? You are right…you! When you demonstrate interest in what the teacher is interested in (the class material), he or she will demonstrate interest in you (in your grade).

❖ ❖ ❖ ❖ ❖ ❖ ❖ ❖ ❖

## When you demonstrate interest, you will receive interest!

❖ ❖ ❖ ❖ ❖ ❖ ❖ ❖ ❖

We spoke to many high school teachers and compiled a top-ten list of offensive things students have done in class.

- Being late to class and interrupting the lecture
- Talking and distracting others while the teacher is talking
- Falling asleep in class
- Reading a magazine or newspaper in class
- Propping up smelly feet
- Putting on nail polish in class
- Hanky-panky between a girlfriend and boyfriend during the lecture
- Playing music through headphones
- Text Messaging via a cell phone during class
- Being verbally abusive toward the teacher and other students

You must remember that **teachers are people, too**. Most high school teachers are over-worked and underpaid. Some teachers can easily double their salary by changing jobs. In addition, they spend many long hours in school—often getting there before the students arrive and leaving later, long after students have cleared out. This means, they really care about you and they like to teach. If

> **If you display a lack of interest or disrespectful behavior in class, teachers will most likely take it personally.**

you display a lack of interest or disrespectful behavior in class, teachers will most likely take it personally. The principle is simple—**when you demonstrate interest, you will receive interest!**

✦ ✦ ✦ ✦ ✦ ✦ ✦ ✦ ✦

## *3 secrets about your teachers:*
### 2. Teacher = Friend
• **See teachers off-line to receive more info**

✦ ✦ ✦ ✦ ✦ ✦ ✦ ✦ ✦

Ok, I can almost hear the sarcastic chuckles. "Friend? Yeah, right! I don't see myself hanging out with my teacher!" Allow me to define "friend" in this context. A friend is someone who cares about your well-being. Here is the key: **the teacher wants to help you learn!** Since you want to learn as well, this is the perfect common ground between you and the teacher.

Interestingly, I learned this lesson when I was in the 2nd grade. I have 3 brothers and sisters and we were often on the honor roll in school. The school would print our names in a newspaper, and my proud mother would take the paper to church to show it to everybody. However, that first marking period in 2nd grade, I missed the A honor roll as well as the B honor roll (although I had A's in all academic subjects) because the teacher gave me a C in conduct. The teacher wrote a comment on the report card that I "can't sit there and be still and be quiet."

Remember my "old school" mother from the time management section? Well, the C in conduct was not acceptable to her, so she "communicated." Again, she was never abusive but her discipline was definitely memorable. She coupled her physical communication with the verbal warning "if you want to live… in my house…" and "anyone should be able to sit in class and be still and be quiet even if you can't do the assignment."

Even though I was only in 2nd grade, I knew it was impossible for me to sit in the class and be still and be quiet. (I am naturally very active; if medication had been more popular, I probably would have been on Ritalin.) However, I also had the "FEAR OF MY MOTHER" in me so I had to figure out a compromise. I found out quickly that there was one person in the classroom that I could talk to "all day, everyday" and not get in trouble. I used my energy and became engaged in class as well. I became a teacher's pet out of necessity... I WANTED TO LIVE!

All jokes aside, I learned something very valuable through that experience that still applies today. **When you see teachers off-line, they will share more information with you than they could in class.** Have you ever talked to a teacher outside of class and heard this type of subtle hint: "make sure you study this for the exam"? There are many other benefits to having a teacher as a friend. When you utilize TOH, you can quickly develop a relationship. In short, your teacher becomes someone who is interested in seeing you succeed in the class.

> **By the way, don't expect the teacher to do your homework for you by asking questions on every single problem!**

**Another case in point, a 10th grade student shared the following experience.**

"I followed the Guaranteed A+ PLUS Plan and saw my teacher outside of class to ask questions. One week, I was really sick and missed a major test in U.S. history. I was really worried because the teacher is known for giving really difficult make-up tests. I showed him the doctor's note and explained why I missed the test. He listened patiently and said that he knew I would not purposely miss class. Instead of the ultra-hard make-up test, he gave me the regular exam. I ended up Acing that history test!"

Some people think that the student just got plain lucky. I believe that the student received favor in the situation because of her weekly meetings with her teacher. The teacher got to know her personally and therefore was willing to help her more than usual! **This is the power of a teacher's red pen!** Have you ever wondered about the difference between two students who both got 89% in the same class and one received a B and the other student got an A?

If you are going to have a friend in the classroom, doesn't it pay to have the teacher on your side?

❖ ❖ ❖ ❖ ❖ ❖ ❖ ❖ ❖

### *3 secrets about your teachers:* 3. Teacher is KEY!

❖ ❖ ❖ ❖ ❖ ❖ ❖ ❖ ❖

I learned this principle from my grandmother; we called her "Mama Pearle." As you may recall from chapter 2, my mother is very "old school." But Mama Pearle was old school in a different way. She never communicated physically, because she never had to. Her verbal communication was mild, concise, and infrequent. (I think she could go a whole day without saying a word!) She spoke up when her wisdom was needed. Though few, her instructions were golden and followed without question! She actually lived to be 100 years old, and in my lifetime I never heard my grandmother repeat herself!

When I was in the third grade, I told Mama Pearle that I did not want to go back to school because I hated my teacher. My grandmother looked straight at me and said:

> "Donna,
> Tomorrow, you are going to school.
> Tomorrow when you go to school,
> your objective is not to like your teacher.
> Your objective is to learn everything that she knows.
> When you master the concepts in the 3rd grade,
> you will be ready for the 4th grade.
> And, when you master the concepts in the 4th grade,
> you will be ready for the 5th grade.
> And, when you master the concepts in the 5th grade,
> you will be ready for the 6th grade, 7th grade and 8th grade…"

Step by step, she took this speech all the way to graduate school! Then she said "and that is what you are going to do tomorrow." At the end, all I said was: "Yes, Mama Pearle." When I went to school the next day, my whole focus had changed. My objective was no longer to like my teacher or for her to like me. It was to get into my teacher's head and learn all that she knew so I could go on to the next grade. I made all A's and eventually grew to appreciate my teacher.

You are not always going to like all of your teachers. There are different teaching and learning styles. Sometimes, students mentally "check out" in class or stop going altogether because they do not like a certain teacher. In the end, you are the only one being hurt by that decision. **Teachers have what you need to move on to the next level!** Should you let a teacher hinder your grade and ultimately throw away your money? Your job is to get firsthand information. The teacher is the key to your learning and your grade! Bottom line, the teacher is the bottom line. Even if your teacher is not your friend, he or she is still the key to your success!

✦ ✦ ✦ ✦ ✦ ✦ ✦ ✦ ✦

### *3 secrets about your teachers:*

### 3. Teacher is KEY…
- to my learning!
- to my grade!

✦ ✦ ✦ ✦ ✦ ✦ ✦ ✦ ✦

# Step 2 Review

**Why and when should I go see my teacher?**
- To get firsthand information
- During Teacher's Office Hours (TOH)
  - Before school, after school or by appointment

**Need a starting point?**
- Discuss corrected homework/exam problems
- Explain a concept to your teacher

**3 Secrets about your Teacher**
1. Teachers are people, too!
   - When you demonstrate interest, you will receive interest!

2. Teacher = Friend
   - See teachers off-line to receive more info

3. Teacher is the KEY!
   - Key to my learning!
   - Key to my grade!

## <u>Guaranteed A+ PLUS Exercise</u>

|  | Name of Class | Write down the best TOH for each class |
|---|---|---|
| Class 1 |  |  |
| Class 2 |  |  |
| Class 3 |  |  |
| Class 4 |  |  |
| Class 5 |  |  |
| Class 6 |  |  |
|  |  |  |
|  |  |  |

# Step 3: A Proven Method for Academic Success

This step is the most important key to the Guaranteed A+ PLUS Learning System. On the A+ PLUS Plan, you can easily reduce study time and boost your grades by doing what you are supposed to do when you are supposed to do it. We will show you exactly how to DO IT IN ORDER in this step.

## *STEP 3: Do It In Order!*

We all follow a certain order to accomplish some of the most basic things in life every day. Think back to when you first learned how to tie your shoelaces. You probably learned similar step-by-step instructions as I did:

Hold the ends of the shoelace, one in each hand
Cross one over another and gently pull it tight
Let one end go and make a loop with the other
Wrap the second end around the first loop and make another loop
Carefully pull it through and make it tight
This is how you tie your shoelace!

When children don't tie their shoes in the order instructed, they often come untied and have to be redone. It is the same with learning! When we don't approach learning in a systematic order, it takes extra time and energy and we often have to re-learn material that was forgotten.

## *What are you supposed to do before going to class?*

The answer is simple: "READ!" There is an old saying: "Reading Is Fundamental (RIF)." A cliché; nonetheless, it is still true. Reading the assigned materials before going to class causes you to become familiar with the terms in the book, so it will be easier to understand the teacher during class.

It is just like seeing a movie twice. The second time you see it, it is easier to understand and remember more details. When you read the material that will be covered in class, at least 1 day prior to class, you will be able to compre-hend a lot more of the information during class.

> **Remember, doing the A+ Plus Plan in order can cut your study time in half!**

Because you now understand the class material, your homework will not take as long as before. **Snap, Guaranteed A+ PLUS just cut your study time!**

## *The real question is: Do you remember what you read???*

In Guaranteed A+ PLUS seminars, I often bet the students $100 that most of them don't know how to read. To prove my point, I ask: "How many people have ever read a chapter, closed the book, and did not remember anything that was just read?"

Almost all students admit that it happens all the time! The purpose of reading is to gain information, so you can use it later. If you cannot even remember, you are not really reading! Also, it will be very difficult to use the information in future classes, homework or exams. Guaranteed A+ PLUS's reading method can save a great deal of time because you will actually remember the material, and avoid re-reading!

✦ ✦ ✦ ✦ ✦ ✦ ✦ ✦ ✦ ✦

### *Bullet Point Reading (BPR)*
### Read to Remember!

✦ ✦ ✦ ✦ ✦ ✦ ✦ ✦ ✦ ✦

Our reading method is so powerful, if you just read the "A+ PLUS way," you can earn at least a B average or a 3.0 GPA. However, this is the Guaranteed A+ PLUS Learning System, so we are going to stay on plan for straight A's!

Let's say you're reading chapter 5 of a textbook that has been divided into 10 sections. Follow the BPR process.

1. **Continue reading** (in Section 1)

2. **Stop** (each time you see an important thought, concept, or definition)

3. **Summarize it in 3-5 words** (on a <u>separate sheet of lined paper</u>).

> **Please don't simply depend on your memory for these bullet points. You can't remember them all. Make sure you write them down on a separate sheet of paper.**

Now continue reading until you come to the next important part, stop reading and summarize it in 3-5 words. Keep reading until you come to the next important fact, stop reading and summarize it in 3-5 words. Repeat this process until the end of section 1.

| Class ABC, Chapter 5 |
| --- |
| Section 1 |
| • Hey Hey Hey Hey |
| |
| • La La La La La |
| |

**When you've finished reading section 1, you have essentially made a bullet-point outline of this section.** Now, you simply REVIEW all the bullet points created from section 1.

| Class ABC, Chapter 5 |
|---|
| Section 1 |
| • Hey Hey Hey Hey |
| |
| • La La La La La |
| |

REVIEW BPR
(Section 1)

Now, we can move on to section two and repeat the same **Bullet Point Reading (BPR)** procedure:

1. **Continue reading** (in Section 2)

2. **Stop** (each time you see an important thought, concept, or definition)

3. **Summarize it in 3-5 words**

When you finish doing section 2's BPR, it is time to REVIEW! Go all the way back to the top of section 1 and **review all the bullet points in sections 1 and 2**.

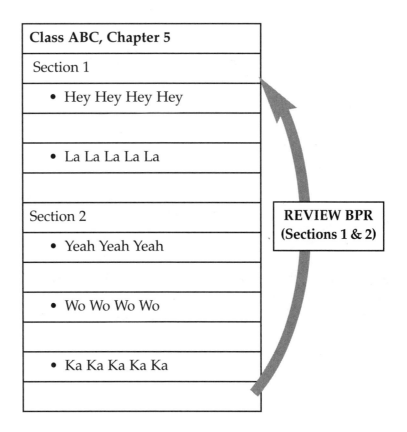

| Class ABC, Chapter 5 |
|---|
| Section 1 |
| • Hey Hey Hey Hey |
| |
| • La La La La La |
| |
| Section 2 |
| • Yeah Yeah Yeah |
| |
| • Wo Wo Wo Wo |
| |
| • Ka Ka Ka Ka Ka |
| |

REVIEW BPR
(Sections 1 & 2)

After reviewing from the top, continue to BPR in section 3. What should you do at the end of section 3? You guessed correctly! **Review all the bullet points from sections 1, 2, and 3.** The process for these first 3 sections will look like this:

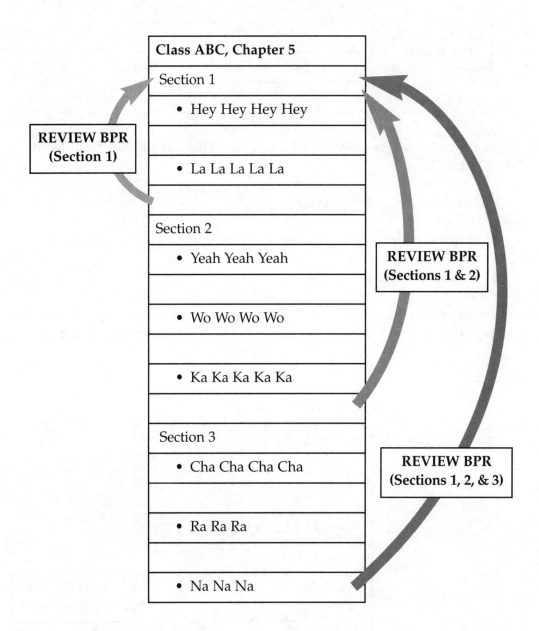

Keep repeating this process until you are finished with section 10. You will have reviewed bullet points from section 1 a total of 10 times! When you follow the BPR process, information you read won't simply vanish into thin air!

✦ ✦ ✦ ✦ ✦ ✦ ✦ ✦ ✦

## *Definition of Bullet Point*
### 3-5 words that summarize an important thought, concept, or definition.

✦ ✦ ✦ ✦ ✦ ✦ ✦ ✦ ✦

### *Remember your ABC's?*

Remember the ABC song from your childhood? If I start singing *"A.B.C.D.,"* what is next? I am sure you are probably humming in your head: *"E.F.G."* What if I continue with *"H.I.J.K."*? You will reply with: *"L.M.N.O.P."* Great job...you remember your ABC's!

Why do you remember the ABC song? I bet you did not sing it last night just for fun (unless you have younger family members who are learning their ABC's). I use the ABC song to illustrate a very important principle. You learned the alphabet because you repeated the song over and over (and over). It's all about repetition, which engraves the material into your long-term memory. Herein lies the most important Guaranteed A+ PLUS Principle—**Strategic Repetition over a period of time puts things into long-term memory.**

We were taught our alphabets in repeating segments. Ever notice how everyone always groups "A, B, C, D" together before moving on to "E, F, G"? It's because we were taught to repeat those letters in that same pattern: ABCD, ABCD, ABCD, — EFG, EFG, EFG. (Is the ABC song in your head yet?)

✦ ✦ ✦ ✦ ✦ ✦ ✦ ✦ ✦

## *Guaranteed A+ PLUS Principle*
### Strategic Repetition ⟶ Long-term Memory

✦ ✦ ✦ ✦ ✦ ✦ ✦ ✦ ✦

BPR breaks the material down into 3-5 words that are easy to remember. **The bullet points from Section 1 are equivalent to an "ABCD" segment. The bullet points from Section 2 are equivalent to a "EFG" segment, and so on.** When you do BPR and review from the beginning of section 1, you are actively using the principle of repetition and putting the material into long-term memory. **BPR should be done at least 1 to 7 days before your class, giving the information enough time to sink in through repetition.**

---

**Please note: Bullet points can be done more than 1 day before going to class. If you do BPR more than 1 day prior to class, simply review it right before class to refresh your memory.**

---

✦ ✦ ✦ ✦ ✦ ✦ ✦ ✦ ✦

### *Bullet Point Reading (BPR)*

- **At least 1-7 days before class**
- **Continue reading**
- **Stop**
- **Summarize in 3-5 words**

✦ ✦ ✦ ✦ ✦ ✦ ✦ ✦ ✦

As shown by the example, **you should also skip a line between bullet points**. Visually, it is a lot easier to read BPs and review quickly when you skip a line between each BP. By reviewing BPs from different sections, your brain is learning the material as you would learn the ABC song—by repeating segments. In short, by using the BPR concept, **you'll read to remember.**

## *What are the 3 benefits of BPR?*

"Bullet point reading" has three main benefits. **First, BPR helps you to pay attention.** Now you are reading actively with purpose because you have to do something as a result of what you are reading. Therefore, you can easily focus your attention on the task of reading. You won't get to page 5 and realize you have just been calling words since page 2, and have to reread everything.

Second, **BPR puts the information in your own words**. It is easier to remember your own words than someone else's. Material in your own words is familiar, comfortable, and easier to understand.

The brain remembers information best when it is in clusters of 3-7 components. When the information has more than 7 words or components, the brain has to gear up to another level and then divides the information into smaller units in order to make meaning. This can impede the learning process by making it longer. This is the third benefit: **BPR provides a concise "brain-friendly" information format that can easily be reviewed repetitiously.** When doing BPR, you break the information up once and for all. It will now take less brain-processing time each time you review the material.

✦ ✦ ✦ ✦ ✦ ✦ ✦ ✦ ✦

### *3 Benefits of BPR*

- **Helps you to pay attention**
- **Puts info in your own words**
- **Provides "Brain-friendly" concise format**
  - Reviewed repetitiously
  - Easily reviewed & remembered

✦ ✦ ✦ ✦ ✦ ✦ ✦ ✦ ✦

## *Here are some examples of the BPR process.*

### BPR Example #1

The set of real numbers contains all positive numbers, all negative numbers, and zero. Real numbers can be represented as points on a number line. You have made and used number lines in earlier mathematics courses by marking off equal distances from a starting point, labeled 0. The zero point is also called the **origin**. Numbers to the right of 0 are called **positive** numbers and numbers to the left of 0 are called **negative** numbers. Zero (0) is neither positive nor negative.

### Example (Student A)

| |
|---|
| • **Real # = positive + negative + 0** |
| |
| • **0 = origin** |
| |
| • **0 ⟶ not positive, not negative** |

### Example (Student B) Another student chose to do this BPR pictorially:

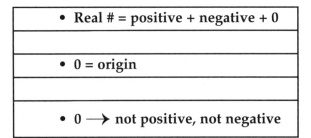

### BPR Example #2

### Chapter 2, Section 2-1

It is a boom time for college hoppers. Since the 1970s, the number of four-year and community college students who transfer at least once before graduation has risen from 47 percent to 60 percent of all graduates, says the U. S. Department of Education. The change is due to a 70s legislation passed by Congress to shift financial aid from institutions to individuals. As a result, this law created a generation of students with money to shop around. Just as American workers are now quicker to change jobs, students are quicker to change schools.

| |
|---|
| • **Transfer student increase** |
| • Since 70's, 47 ⟶ 60% |
| |
| • **Reason: $ follows student** |

### BPR Example #3: Invention of Post-it ® notes

Post-it ® notes may have been a Godsend…literally. In the early 1970s, Art Fry was in search of a bookmark for his church hymnal that would neither fall out nor damage the hymnal. Fry noticed that a colleague at 3M, Dr. Spencer Silver, had developed an adhesive that was strong enough to stick to surfaces, but left no residue after removal and could be repositioned. Fry took some of Dr. Silver's adhesive and applied it along the edge of a piece of paper. His church hymnal problem was solved!

Fry soon realized that his "bookmark" had other potential functions when he used it to leave a note on a work file, and coworkers kept dropping by, seeking "bookmarks" for their offices. This "bookmark" was a new way to communicate and to organize. 3M Corporation crafted the name Post-it note for Fry's bookmarks and began production in the late 70's for commercial use.

In 1977, test-markets failed to show consumer interest. However in 1979, 3M implemented a massive consumer sampling strategy, and the Post-it note took off. Today, we see Post-it ® notes peppered across files, computers, desks, and doors in offices and homes throughout the country. From a church hymnal bookmark to an office and home essential, the Post-it note has really changed the way we work.

### BPR Example (Student A)

| |
|---|
| • Hymnal bookmark, Art Fry |
| |
| • Paper w/ Spencer Silver's special glue |
| |
| • 3M named "Post-it note" |
| |
| • Commercial use = late 70's |
| |
| • 1977 – test-markets failed |
| |
| • 1979 – massive sampling strategy = took off |
| |

## BPR Example (Student B)

| |
|---|
| • Post-it Notes |
|    • Early 70's, Art Fry's idea |
|    • + 3M colleague, Dr. Spencer Silver |
|    • Removable glue with no residue |
|    • '79 give samples → successful |

## BPR Example #4

### Principle-Based Leadership Case Study
### Chick-fil-A Corporation

The Sunday night gathering of Chick-fil-A employees and their family members in downtown Salt Lake City had all the makings of a church service. About 100 people, most dressed in their Sunday best, started the evening with a prayer, then listened as a Chick-fil-A employee sang a couple of Christian songs. Then, Chick-fil-A president Dan Cathy took the stage, focusing on Christianity's role in the everyday business of a fast-food restaurant chain.

"My pulpit is 20-feet wide and operates six days a week," he said, referring to countertops at each restaurant location. He detailed the company's growth in a speech peppered with scripture. He also laid out the company's mission statement: "to glorify God by being a faithful steward of all that is entrusted to us and to have a positive influence on all who come in contact with Chick-fil-A."

Cathy makes no excuses for his dedication to God. Indeed, he believes Christian principles have helped propel the growth of his business built by his father. The energetic 49-year-old Georgia native says he would rather be able to quote Jesus Christ than Jack Welch. He carries around a small copy of the New Testament instead of the popular business book, *"Who Moved My Cheese?"* But make no mistake: the Cathy family knows how to run a business.

Dan Cathy's father, Truett, opened the first Chick-fil-A in Atlanta. The chain steadily grew for years, expanding all over the nation without compromising Cathy's Christian principles. The most visible component of the chain's spiritual conviction is its "Closed on Sundays" policy: all of the chain's restaurants are closed on Sunday to allow employees time with their families and time to worship, if they desire.

About 20 years ago, Cathy was facing external pressure to abandon his "Closed on Sunday" and other Christianity-based business practices. Their "Closed on Sunday" policy has cost the company deals with Disney, Six Flags, sports stadiums and malls. Cathy could have decided to give in and open his restaurants seven days a week to increase profits. Instead the company chose to stay true to its mission statement and focus on improving technology and menu selections.

According to Dan Cathy, his decision to stay true to Christian principles has paid off. Chick-fil-A is the nation's third largest fast-food chicken restaurant. The chain has 1073 restaurants in 36 states. In 2001, it reported sales of $1.2 billion. The chain on average is opening a new restaurant every week. And recently it was ranked No. 1 in a trade magazine's annual report as having the best drive-through service in America. Of all his business accomplishments, Cathy is most proud of Chick-fil-A's scholarship programs, which have awarded more than fourteen thousand $1,000 scholarships in the last 53 years, totaling over 14 million dollars.

## Sample BPR for this case study

Refer to the chart on the next page. Please note: As the arrows indicate, the student reviewed in the middle of BPR and again at the very end. When there are no clearly defined sections in your reading, simply review periodically as you see fit while doing BPR.

## Chick-fil-A Case Study (BPR)

- Dan Cathy – President

- Pulpit = restaurant countertops

- Mission Statement
    - Glorify God / Faithful Steward
    - Positive influence → All

- Believe Christian principles propel business
    - Rather quote JC than Welch
    - N.T., instead business book

- First restaurant @ Atlanta
    - Opened by Truett Cathy

- "Closed on Sunday" → worship & family time

- Stick w/ principles while under pressure

- Company focus → improvement
    - Technology & menu selection

- Decision = paid off

- 3rd largest chicken fast-food restaurant
    - 1073 location / 36 states
    - 1.2 billion sales (2001)
    - #1 drive-through in US
    - $14 mil. Scholarship in 53 yrs.

**REVIEW BPR (Section 1)**

**REVIEW BPR (Sections 1 & 2)**

## Section Review—3.1

Since we have just learned about Bullet Points, let's use them to summarize the important information in this section.

- **Bullet Point—Definition**
  - 3-5 word summary
  - Important thought, concept, definition

- **Bullet Point Reading (BPR)**
  - 1-7 days before class
  - Continue reading
  - Stop
  - Summarize, 3-5 words
  - Repeat...Finish section
  - Review from section 1

- **BPR on lined paper**
  - Skip lines between BPs

- **A+PLUS Principle:**
  - **Strategic Repetition → Long-term Memory**

- **3 Benefits of BPR**
  - Helps you pay attention
  - Info → my own words
  - "Brain-friendly" concise format
    - Review repetitiously
    - Review & remember

## Guaranteed A+ PLUS Exercises

- Practice with the BPR examples in your workbook

## *What About my Math or Science Class?*

All over the country, students always ask me: **"Will BPR work for formulas?"** The answer is: "Absolutely." The Guaranteed A+ PLUS Learning System was originally created as an engineer's approach to learning. You can use the same system to deal with formulas!

Almost all math and science classes use formulas of some sort. **Have you ever had an exam question that could easily be solved by one of the 20 formulas you learned?** The only problem was that you did not know which formula to pull out of the hat. If you follow the BP format for equations, you will never again wonder what formula to use. Instead of beating your brains out to memorize formulas the night before exams, you can easily learn how to apply the formulas.

---

### Bullet Point Process for Math and Science Formulas

**When doing a BP on a formula, follow these steps:**

1. **Write down the equation**

2. **BP each variable**
   - List each symbol & its meaning separately
   - Include common units in parenthesis (if applicable)

3. **Do summarizing BP(s)**
   - Ask yourself the following questions
     - To use this formula:
       - What *conditions* must be met?
       - What must be *true*?
       - What are the *limitations*?
   - Write down answer(s) as summarizing BP(s)

---

Let's look at one simple math formula: the area of a triangle. Using the BPR method, we will bullet point each symbol in the formula along with its common units.

**A= ½ x b x h**
- **A = area ($cm^2$)**
- **b = base (cm)**
- **h = height (cm)**

**You want to know the common units to increase your familiarity of the formula.** This can also help you avoid potential frustration. You do not want to go through all the calculations for a math or science problem only to find that units were not properly converted prior to the calculation.

Now, take one more step in analyzing the formula. Write the summarizing bullet points. **Summarizing bullet points tell the right conditions to use the formula.** As you can see in the example below, you can have more than one summarizing bullet point.

### Example #1 BPR - Math / Science Formulas

**A= ½ x b x h**
- A = area (cm²)
- b = base (cm)
- h = height (cm)
→ **b ⊥ h OR (b perpendicular to h)**
→ **b & h, same units**

$\boxed{\textbf{Summarizing BPs}}$

These summarizing bullet points become extremely critical when you are doing homework or exams. **These bullet points give you important clues concerning when and how to use each formula.** As a result, you will remember which formula to use during exams with ease.

### Example 1: Area of Circle

$A = \pi r^2$
- A = Area of a circle (cm²)
- π = 3.14
- r = radius of circle (cm)
→ Use Radius, not Diameter

$\boxed{\textbf{Summarizing BPs}}$

### Example 2: Slope of Line

Here is an example from a math textbook:

The slope of a line is a number that describes its steepness. It is the ratio of the changes in y (rise) to the change in x (run). The slope, m, of the line joining any two points (x1, y1 ) and (x2, y2) in the xy-plane is given by:

$$m = \frac{(y_2 - y_1)}{(x_2 - x_1)}$$

Using the equation, the slope of the line joining (-3,-1) and (1, 5) is

$$m = \frac{(y_2 - y_1)}{(x_2 - x_1)} = \frac{(5 - (-1))}{(1 - (-3))} = \frac{6}{4} = \frac{3}{2}$$

## Example Bullet Points (Student A)

$$m = \frac{(y_2 - y_1)}{(x_2 - x_1)}$$

- m = slope / line steepness
- $x_1$ = x-coordinate, point 1
- $y_1$ = y-coordinate, point 1
- $x_2$ = x-coordinate, point 2
- $y_2$ = y-coordinate, point 2
→ Line must join two points

**Summarizing BPs**

## Example Bullet Points (Student B) – familiar with XY coordinates

$$m = \frac{(y_2 - y_1)}{(x_2 - x_1)}$$

- m = slope
- $(y_2 - y_1)$ = change in rise: y-coordinates
- $(x_2 - x_1)$ = change in run: x-coordinates
→ 2 points, XY plane
  → Straight line

**Summarizing BPs**

## Example 3: Chemistry

$P_1 V_1 = P_2 V_2$
- $P_1$ = Initial Pressure (mmHg)
- $V_1$ = Initial Volume (ml)
- $P_2$ = Final Pressure (mmHg)
- $V_2$ = Final Volume (ml)
→ **Ideal gas @ constant temperature**

**Summarizing BPs**

In Part 2 of this book (FAQ #8), Y.C. Chen will offer additional tips on how to deal with multi-step math problems on the A+ PLUS plan.

# Classroom Behavior Demystified

BPR prepares you to understand more of the teacher's lecture, but there are some other unwritten classroom rules that you need to know as well. These also will help in retaining information. Since you are paying for every class, you might as well get all your money's worth. There are three things that you need to do in class on the Guaranteed A+ PLUS plan.

## 1. Be Alert, Focused and Attentive

Simply put, you need to be alert, focused and attentive during class. Generally, the more physically alert you are, the more attentive you will be mentally.

**Sometimes, our body language can get us in trouble during class.** For example, some students are accustomed to slouching in their seats or using their hands to prop their heads up while they may be fully alert, focused and attentive. In reality, this type of body language is only a habit. Most people are not even aware of their actions. **However, to your instructors, this type of body language screams, "I am not interested!"**

The best way to avoid any misunderstanding is to watch what you do in class. Always sit up straight in class, and avoid laying your head on your hand. Again, these things are just habits. Habits can either be broken or reformed. The truth is, at this age, you actually don't need your hand to hold your head up—smile. If you must use your hands to prop up your head, try using fingers—it can actually give you a more interested and intellectual look than before. (smile)

Here is another secret that can significantly increase your grade and reduce stress: **Don't Pack Up Early!** I could tell you that it is rude and disrespectful to the teacher. However, that may not be enough to change your mind. **Here is the real deal: you may miss information that can boost your grades** when you pack up early or mentally check out toward the end of class. For example, a teacher looked at his watch and realized that he only had 5 –10 minutes left in class. He then remembered that the exam was already written and all the necessary material had not been covered during class. So, in the remaining few minutes, the teacher quickly went over critical material that was on the exam. If you had packed up early in this class, you could have easily missed the goodies (i.e. exam material) that could have possibly boosted your grade!

## 2. Be an Active Participant

Another way to learn more in class is to be an active participant. Asking and answering questions and volunteering represent active participation. In addition, this shows your teachers that you are interested. You can increase your attention span and information retention by actively involving yourself in class.

Many times, students don't want to ask questions because they are afraid of looking stupid. If this is a fear of yours, simply remember this tip. **If you have a question during a lecture, most likely 1/3 of the class has the same or a similar question regarding the subject matter.** By raising your hand and asking the question, you will receive the correct answer firsthand from the teacher. Also, you will help other students in the classroom!

## 3. Take Accurate Notes

Accurate notes are not an exact record of the teacher's words. Have you ever attempted to write down everything a teacher said word for word? It becomes a mindless activity. Most students end up with many incomplete sentences and still have no clue regarding the content being taught. The Guaranteed A+ PLUS procedure for taking accurate notes is: **listen first, understand the concept, and then write it down**.

Most teachers introduce one principle at a time during class. They will then explain further with examples or various demonstrations. **This "principle / example" cycle can run a couple of times during a typical class**. This is where your BPR comes in handy; since you are already familiar with the terms and information, it becomes easier to pay attention and understand the teacher. When the teacher gives different examples to support the principle, you will not mistake them as separate ideas and become confused. BPR makes the note-taking process a whole lot easier.

✦ ✦ ✦ ✦ ✦ ✦ ✦ ✦ ✦

## Three Things in Class

- Be Alert, Focused & Attentive
- Be an Active Participant
- Take Accurate Notes
  - Listen first
  - Understand the concept
  - Write it down

✦ ✦ ✦ ✦ ✦ ✦ ✦ ✦ ✦

## *What should I do with my class notes?*

In this section, we are going to cover the secret to organizing class notes—Bullet Point Notes (BPN). So far, you have learned about Bullet Point Reading (BPR at least 1-7 days before class), and the three things you should do in class. Now, I want to show you what you should do after a class. Immediately after a class lecture or after school, you should do a bullet point outline of your class notes. **The process is called Bullet Point Notes (BPN).**

✦ ✦ ✦ ✦ ✦ ✦ ✦ ✦ ✦

## Bullet Point Notes (BPN)

- Immediately after class
- Continue reading (page 1 of your class notes)
- Stop
- Summarize, 3-5 words (on a separate sheet of paper)

✦ ✦ ✦ ✦ ✦ ✦ ✦ ✦ ✦

BPN is done immediately after a class lecture or the end of the school day depending on your high school schedule. Sometimes the teachers will leave time at the end of the class to let you get started on homework assignments. (It is especially true if you are on a block schedule.) Please use this time to BPN before you start your homework. If your teacher takes the entire class hour to teach, you will simple BPN at the end of the school day for all the classes.

> **BPN after a lecture if your teachers give you time for homework during class. If not, simply BPN at the end of the school day for all classes BEFORE starting your homework!**

**BPN uses the same basic process as BPR.** While reading over page 1 of your class notes, summarize each important thought, concept and definition in 3-5 words. When you are finished with BPN for page 1 of your notes, go back and review all the bullet points created from page 1. **Remember to BPN on a separate sheet of paper.**

| Class ABC, 10/10/05 (BPN) |
|---|
| Page 1 |
| • Yeah der hey |
| |
| • Hmm Hmm Hmm |
| |

REVIEW BPN
Page 1

Now, do your bullet point notes for page 2. When you are finished with page 2 BPN, go back and review all BPN from pages 1 and 2.

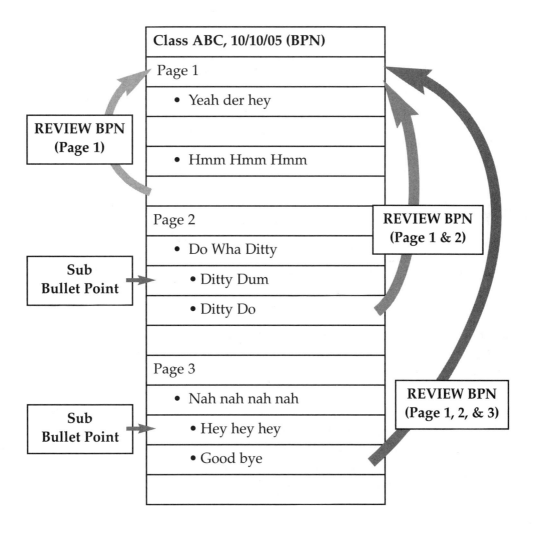

You may notice that BPN for pages 2 and 3 look different than for page 1. These are **Sub Bullet Points.** Whenever you have information that takes more than 5 words to summarize, simply use a heading and put the related information as sub bullet points below it. You may have multiple sub bullet points. Please note that you should **not** skip lines between sub bullet points. This is done to keep and organize related material together in the brain.

---

- Headline + Related information
  - = Sub Bullet Point
  - (Don't skip line)

---

**Now, we are *not* asking you to rewrite all of your notes.** That would take too much time. While most of your lecture notes contain important information, a teacher may teach a major principle and then use several examples to clarify. In this case, simply do a BPN on the major principle and possibly 1 or 2 examples to refresh your memory. **BPN usually takes about 5-10 minutes for an hour of class.**

**Sometimes, students tell me, "BPN is just too much work."** (It is ok to admit it if you had the same thought while reading.) I often reply by asking another question: "have you ever sat in class and thought you understood the material, only to find out you had no clue how to do the homework?" Most students admit the truth sheepishly. BPN will cut your study time by allowing you to identify the part of the lesson you understand and sort out the part where you may need additional information. You will not end up in a situation where you are staring at the textbook and wondering what the teacher said in class.

> **During class, take notes as you usually do and don't try to take class notes in BP form. Only do BPN at the end of a class lecture or after school!**

## Why should I BPN immediately after a class lecture or after school?

It is extremely important to start BPN immediately after a lecture. **It helps to capture the material while it's still fresh in your memory.** The probability of retaining information greatly increases the sooner you repeat it.

For example, it is common after meeting someone to forget his or her name. But, if you immediately repeat the name after meeting that person or write it down, you'll be much more likely to remember it. The A+ PLUS learning system allows you to see the same material several times in different ways. If you have a schedule conflict and cannot BPN immediately after class, please do so as soon as possible that day.

BPN will reinforce the various concepts you learned in class. Who knows? You may even discover that you understand a lot more than you thought. By realizing this early on and utilizing your teacher's office hours (TOH), **you will have confidence and a much easier time completing your homework and exams later.**

## *The Sequence of the A+ Plus Plan*

If you haven't noticed yet, we are **systematically** going through a particular sequence of events. To summarize in a timeline, the process looks like this so far.

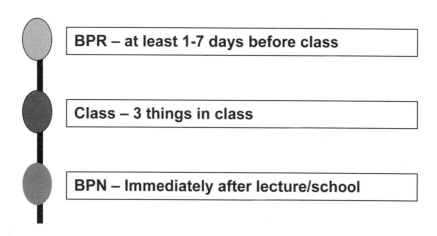

**BPR – at least 1-7 days before class**

**Class – 3 things in class**

**BPN – Immediately after lecture/school**

## Section Review—3.2

### Bullet Point Process – Math / Science Formulas

1. **Write down the equation**

2. **BP each variable**
   - List each symbol & its meaning separately
   - Include common units in parenthesis (if applicable)

3. **Do summarizing BP(s)**
   - Ask yourself the following questions
     - To use this formula:
       - What <u>conditions</u> must be met?
       - What must be <u>*true*</u>?
       - What are the <u>*limitations*</u>?
   - Write down answer(s) as summarizing BP(s)

- **3 things while in class**
  1) Alert, Focused & Attentive
  2) Active Participant
  3) Accurate Notes: Listen, Understand, Write

## *Help! I procrastinate!*

✦ ✦ ✦ ✦ ✦ ✦ ✦ ✦ ✦

### *Guaranteed A+ PLUS says:*
### Simply start your homework the day it is assigned!

✦ ✦ ✦ ✦ ✦ ✦ ✦ ✦ ✦

In the Guaranteed A+ PLUS system, **you will start your homework the DAY it is assigned.** Now, that may sound silly because your homework is usually due the next day anyway. However, have you ever seen "Sam" in homeroom in the morning frantically trying to finish his homework? Or, maybe you knew "David" who was trying to do his homework for the French class during Geometry? (If I am describing you, don't freak out. Just keep on reading and pretend you have never done this before…SMILE.) This kind of unnecessary drama can be easily avoided by **starting** homework the day it is assigned.

Sometimes, students tell us that they stay up all night doing homework. That does not make any sense at all! They waste 50% of the night trying to stay awake by drinking coffee, jolt cola or whatever. They then spend another 25% of the time talking on the phone or chatting on line looking for the unfortunate soul who will listen to them complain about how much work they have to do. They may even do some work in the last 25% of the night. The sad truth is that at midnight by your body clock, you lose at least 50% of your brain's efficiency and productivity. So you will spend 60 minutes doing something that will typically only take 30 minutes when you are fully rested. In short, "all-nighters" are not worth it!

✦ ✦ ✦ ✦ ✦ ✦ ✦ ✦ ✦

### When should you START your homework?
### The day it is assigned!

### The 10-minute Rule

- Stuck on a homework problem
- More than 10 minutes
- Skip the problem
- Get help (TOH)

✦ ✦ ✦ ✦ ✦ ✦ ✦ ✦ ✦

### The 10-minute Rule

When doing homework, you want to observe the 10-minute rule. Assuming you have done all the things described earlier and **you are still stuck on a homework**

**problem for more than 10 minutes, skip the problem and get help.** If you give a solid 10-minute effort, and still have no clue on how to proceed, you are probably missing something fundamental. So, instead of hurting yourself, you should cut your losses and get some help. You can get help from your parents, another adult, teachers or a tutor. Sometimes a couple of minutes with them can answer all your questions about the homework.

Now, you can see how starting the homework the day it is assigned and the 10-minute rule work hand in hand. When you start your homework early, you have time to practice the 10-minute rule and get help. If you start an assignment at 10 p.m. or the morning it is due, you might have a hard time getting help if you run into any problems.

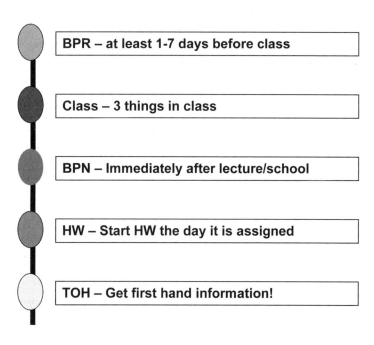

BPR – at least 1-7 days before class

Class – 3 things in class

BPN – Immediately after lecture/school

HW – Start HW the day it is assigned

TOH – Get first hand information!

# Understanding the principles with Bullet Point Concepts (BPC)

## The secret to analyzing homework and exams

Because you are on the A+ PLUS Plan, you actually will finish your homework before it is due. Congratulations, you're ON PLAN! Now, let's talk about the next phase of the plan. What should you do when homework is returned? The same thing you've been doing with everything else, create bullet points. The last type of BP, **Bullet Point Concepts (BPC)**, is the difference between a B and an A+ for most students.

## Importance of BPC

In middle school and some 9th grade classes, getting good grades on tests almost always depends on the student's ability to memorize the material. It is a very different ball game in college-prep classes in the 10th or 11th grade. There may still be part of the test that requires you to memorize and repeat facts and figures learned during lecture or from a textbook. However, more and more emphasis will be placed on critical thinking. Your teachers will start to prepare exams to test the student's ability to apply principles and concepts. They expect you to understand the 'why' behind the concepts and then apply those principles to solve future problems. Doing BPC will ensure you know how to apply your knowledge. That is why we can guarantee you an A+ PLUS when you are ON PLAN!

> **In addition to being the difference between a B and an A+, BPC is also your ultimate secret weapon for SAT/ACT and other standardized test preparation. (See the FAQ #9)**

## How do you BPC?

When you get corrected homework or exams back, **review EACH problem and answer the question: "Why is this the correct answer?"** Have you ever answered a question correctly on a homework problem but you had no idea why it was correct? Would you be able to answer a similar question correctly again on the next test? Probably not. **That is why you need to BPC all problems, not just the ones that were marked wrong.**

You want to understand *why* it's the correct answer and then summarize it in BP format. If a problem is not correct, first find the right answer, and then do your BPC. If you don't know the right answer, you can go to TOH and get help correcting the answers to your homework or exams before you BPC. By doing BPC, you will know the "WHY" behind every single homework problem and question.

Once you have completed and reviewed your BPC, acing similar problems on future homework or tests will be easy!

❖ ❖ ❖ ❖ ❖ ❖ ❖ ❖ ❖

## Bullet Point Concepts (BPC)

- On corrected HW & Exams
- Answers the Question: "WHY?"
- "Why is this the correct answer?"

❖ ❖ ❖ ❖ ❖ ❖ ❖ ❖ ❖

## BPC Example #1 - Math

Let's practice with a really simple math question,

$$1 + 2 \times 3 = ?$$

At first glance, someone may answer 9 by mistake. Actually, 7 is the correct answer. Now to do the BPC on this problem, we have to ask: **"Why is 7 the correct answer?"**

We may answer the question several ways and each answer can be a BPC.

- **Order of operations**
- **Multiply 1st, Add 2nd**
- **P.E.M.D.A.S.**

Note: P.E.M.D.A.S., also known as "Please Excuse My Dear Aunt Sally," stands for parenthesis, exponents, multiply, divide, add, and subtract.

There are virtually unlimited numbers of combinations for simple math problems like this. You wouldn't memorize the exact math problem for an upcoming test! (Can you imagine how crazy you would feel if you tried to cram $1 + 2 \times 3 = 7$ into your head?) **With BPC, you examine the *why* behind the right answer**. Now you can solve any similar math problems with ease.

## BPC Example #2 - English

Let's look at an English example together. Please choose the correct verb.

**People is / are always speaking incorrectly.**

The answer is "are" for this sentence.

Your BPC may look like one of these:

- **Subject-Verb Agreement**
- **People = Plural → ARE = Plural**

## BPC Example #3 - Chemistry

Why don't we do a more advanced example? Let's say you are taking chemistry and your homework includes knowing the molecular structure of soap. (I use soap for this example because hopefully it is something we are all familiar with.)

Soap works because it has two ends. One end of a soap molecule is hydrophilic. (Hydrophilic means that it likes water.) The other end is hydrophobic; you guessed it, it does not like water! The end that likes water (hydrophilic), attaches to the water coming out of your showerhead. The end that does not like water (hydrophobic), likes dirt and grease. Guess what? It attaches to your skin! The end that likes water is stronger and pulls the other end off your body, along with dirt and grease. Then it all goes down the drain with the rest of the water. Now you can say: "Aha! I know how soap cleanses!"

After you have correctly answered a homework problem about the molecular structure of soap, you are ready to do BPC. You want to know *why* soap works. You can rewrite the molecular structure again just for repetition, but the critical thing is to understand and remember that soap works because it has 2 ends. So, the BPC for soap can simply look like the diagram below:

## SOAP BPC:

### *Benefit of BPC*

When teachers design exams, it is obvious that they can't use the same questions that were on homework or previous quizzes. On the other hand, they still have to test you on the same set of principles those questions were based on.

By doing BPC on each homework and quiz problem, you will be armed with the knowledge of "WHY." Before you know it, you will be better prepared to ace the next test!

Students often ask me in seminars: "What happens if my teacher doesn't return exams?" My classic answer has always been: "Who is your friend? And, who do you see every week?" There are many reasons that your teachers may not return exams. But remember "teacher = friend" and all you have to do is ask. If your teacher is still uneasy about returning an exam, you still have another option. You can always ask your teacher to allow you to review the questions and do BPC during TOH, before or after school. The benefits of understanding the principles on old exams in order to apply them to ace future tests far outweigh any minor inconveniences. By the way, your teacher will most likely be impressed by your persistence and desire to learn as well! This is a win-win situation!

## Section Review -3.3

- **Bullet Point Notes (BPN)**
  - Immediately after a class lecture or school
  - Continue reading
  - Stop
  - Summarize, 3-5 words
  - Repeat…Finish page
  - Review from page 1

- **Homework (HW)**
  - Start, day assigned
  - Avoid unnecessary drama

- **The 10-minute Rule**
  - Stuck on a homework problem
  - More than 10 minutes
  - Skip the problem
  - **Get help (TOH)**

- **Bullet Point Concepts (BPC)**
  - On corrected HW & Exams
  - Answers the Question: WHY
  - WHY is this the correct answer?

- **Benefit of BPC**
  - Understand principles for future application
  - Why vs. What
  - Secret to analyzing Exams / HW
  - Difference between A+ and B

### *A secret weapon to stay on top of it all*
### - Bullet Point Notebook

You have 3 types of Bullet Points: Bullet Point Reading (BPR), Bullet Point Notes (BPN) and Bullet Point Concepts (BPC). **Keep all of your bullet points in a Bullet Point Notebook and take it with you everywhere!** This gives you the flexibility to review BPs at any convenient time. You will still keep other notebooks for your class notes and assignments. **Please note: The only thing in your bullet point notebook should be bullet points.**

◆ ◆ ◆ ◆ ◆ ◆ ◆ ◆ ◆

## Bullet Point Notebook

- Organize all BPs → In 1 Notebook
    - Take it everywhere
    - Review repetitiously

◆ ◆ ◆ ◆ ◆ ◆ ◆ ◆ ◆

You can't carry all of your textbooks with you all the time. But, you can definitely take a BP notebook with you everywhere you go. Your BP notebook gives you a snapshot of all your classes. By having an organized BP notebook, you have all the important info from all classes. Remember, your BPR is an outline of important textbook material. BPN are done on your class notes and BPC covers your returned homework and exams. Now, you are set!

**Take all opportunities to review your BPs.** For example, if your friends were 10 minutes late to meet you, instead of getting upset or twiddling your thumbs, just review BPs! Not only are you not wasting time, but you are also preparing yourself for an A+ PLUS finish.

> **You should keep a separate class binder for your class notes and handouts. Remember, the only thing in your BP notebook should be BPR, BPN, and BPC!**

### How do I organize my BP notebook?

To correctly organize your BP notebook, you need the following material:

- One 3-ring binder (1" or 1 $1/2$")

- 3 dividers with tabs per academic class (So, if you have 6 classes, 18 individual dividers are required.)

- 1 self-adhesive tab per academic class (So, if you have 6 classes…you probably already did the math, 6 tabs are needed.)

For each of your classes, you should have 3 dividers labeled: BPR, BPN, BPC on their vertical tabs. You also need 1 horizontal self-adhesive tab to identify the subject matter. The subject tab should be attached to the first divider for that class, which is BPR.

After repeating the process, you will have a set of dividers labeled BPR, BPN, and BPC for each class. Then put these dividers into the 3-ring binder. Voila, you now have a BP notebook. **You can now put all BPs into their appropriate spots and review them repetitiously!** For your convenience, we have custom dividers with BPR, BPN, BPC already printed on them. (Check out www.NoMoreStudy.com for more details.)

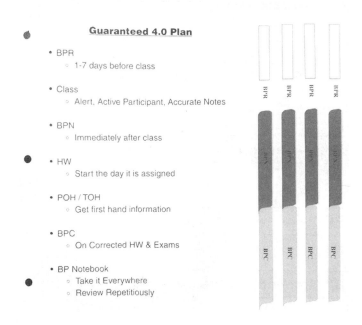

**The BP notebook is your secret weapon to staying ready for quizzes and exams.** Come on, let's face it, all of us have crammed for an exam and done well. But, there is a major drawback to cramming. The information is only retained in short-term memory, soon to be forgotten after the exam. You can end up paying a high price later when you have forgotten the material and are unprepared for a comprehensive exam. There is too much information to cram into your head in such a short period of time. **Using the Guaranteed A+ PLUS Plan, you will never have to cram for an exam again.** Strategic repetition over a period of time puts things into long-term memory! By reviewing repetitiously, you will actually learn the material and be able to remember it. You will be amazed by how easy it will be to prepare for final exams. Studying is a pay me now or pay me later scenario. If you pay now (study now by following the A+ PLUS Plan), you pay less. If you pay later (study later by cramming), you will ultimately end up paying more. I suggest that you pay now and save yourself some time, stress, and money!

**BPR – at least 1-7 days before class**

**Class – 3 things in class**

**BPN – Immediately after lecture/school**

**HW – Start HW the day it is assigned**

**TOH – Get first hand information!**

**BPC – Answers the question "WHY?"**

**BP Notebook – take everywhere – Review**

> **Rule of Thumb for Learning = 3, 60, 24, 7**
> - 3 Seconds
> - 60 Minutes
> - 24 Hours
> - 7 Days

If you don't repeat information the first time you hear it within 3 seconds, you forget it. Remember the first day of school when you met new people, had great conversations, but immediately forgot their names—you didn't repeat their names with 3 seconds. Information has to be repeated within 3 seconds, again within 60 minutes, and again within 24 hours and 7 days to move the information from short-term memory to long-term memory.

The Guaranteed 4.0 system works because it fits the way your brain was created. As you are doing Bullet Point Reading (BPR), when you come to an important point, within 3 seconds you stop and summarize it in 3-5 words. At the end of a section, you go back to the beginning and review. When you do that for each section during the Bullet Point Reading (BPR) process, you have met the 60-minute rule.

When you go to class, hear the information communicated by your teacher, make sure you understand the information and write it down, take accurate notes within 3 seconds of your teacher communicating the information—you have fulfilled the 3-second rule again. At the end of each class, if you do Bullet Point Notes (BPN), you meet the 60-minute rule. Then when you start your homework the day it is assigned, you meet the 24-hour rule. And finally, when you get your homework back, do Bullet Point Concepts (BPC) and TOH, you meet the 7-day rule.

# 3 things about the word "study"

## *That every student should know*

✦ ✦ ✦ ✦ ✦ ✦ ✦ ✦ ✦

### *First thing about study:*

### Study at the same time & same place

✦ ✦ ✦ ✦ ✦ ✦ ✦ ✦ ✦

I actually learned this principle from my former assistant pastor. She presented a series entitled: "Lord, Teach us to Pray!" There was one thing she taught in that series that I never forgot. She said that you need to have a consistent time and consistent place to pray. As a result of that message, I designated a chair in my room as my "prayer chair."

Every time I see that chair, I think about prayer! Every time I sit in that chair, I am praying! Every time I pass by that chair and I have not been in that chair for a while…well, it makes me think that I should be praying. The chair literally represents PRAYER to me! When I sit in that chair, I don't have to get all geared up to pray; food doesn't distract me or telephone calls. When I sit in that chair, my body is already PRE-CONDITIONED to PRAY because that is the only thing I do in that chair!

The same principle applies to studying. **When you establish a consistent time and consistent place to study, you are pre-conditioning your body to study more effectively.** You actually create a habit of studying. A habit is something that you can do that does not require as much conscience thought as other actions. For example, you have a habit of eating. When your favorite meal is placed in front of you, no one has to remind you to pick up your silverware and bring food to your mouth. It is a habit that you do without much conscious thought. Studying also becomes a habit during that specific time and at that particular place.

Be honest with yourself, if you sit down to study for 2 to 3 hours, how long does it usually take you to get into gear? The average answer all over the country is **30-45 minutes** before completely getting into the "zone" of productive studying. But, when you study at the same time and place and are pre-conditioned to study, the results are quite different. **It**

**now only takes 5-10 minutes to engage in productive studying!** Studying at the same time and same place will drastically cut your studying time.

Some students have said: "I don't know if I have the discipline to do that." Guess what? Once you start following the A+ PLUS Plan, your brain will take over and help you! Before you know it, you will have established the routine! For example, remember that plate of your favorite food set before you. You don't have to gear up and teach yourself how to eat again? NO! Your pre-conditioned response is to open your mouth, chew, and swallow and lick your fingers if necessary! It is just that simple. **We are going to make our brains' power work for us!**

✦ ✦ ✦ ✦ ✦ ✦ ✦ ✦ ✦

## *Second thing about study:*
## Study in a quiet place

✦ ✦ ✦ ✦ ✦ ✦ ✦ ✦ ✦

You should study in a quiet place that is conducive to studying. **A conducive place means that it lends itself easily to the act of studying.** There are many places that can be conducive for one student, but totally disastrous for another. Some students study well in the library. My friend Gary could sit in the library and study for 3 hours without moving or being distracted (I can't sit anywhere for more than 15 minutes without distracting myself). The library can be a good choice, although a lot of students sit in the wrong spot in the library. You know, those "social gathering locations" in the library—either by the magazines or internet-enabled PC tables where everyone lingers. Those are not good locations to study. We may start with good intentions to study, however, before long, we find ourselves caught up in conversation, email or watching the latest web video. Those spots are not conducive for studying.

If you stop for a moment and be honest with yourself, you can probably figure out the places that are really good for you to study. **Most of us have difficulties studying in our room because there is just too much to distract us at our fingertips.** There are a couple solutions to this problem:

1) DON'T STUDY THERE! Try another corner of the house, library or school, if possible.

2) ORGANIZE YOUR ROOM. Well, even wishful things can sometimes come true. Please refer to FAQ #15 & 16 for quick and easy tips on keeping your room clean!

As you can see by now, what is conducive can depend on your individual circumstances. So, instead of a discussion on "quiet places to study," I actually want to focus on the places that are not conducive!

Most of us lie to ourselves: *"I just have my TV on for the background noise while I am studying!"* The truth is that if you have the TV on, you generally only remember *during commercial breaks* that you were supposedly studying. This is especially true of your favorite show. Do yourself a favor by being honest, just schedule TV time and watch your favorite show! Let's not pretend to study during that time just to ease a guilty conscience.

*"What about listening to music while reading?"* Here is what generally happens to me (and many other students): my foot starts to tapping, my head and body start to "groove" with the rhythm; instead, before I know it, I grab my imaginary microphone and pollute the air-quality with my off-key singing! As we said before, stress is anything that takes you away from the

task at hand! **Listening to music can take your focus away from studying** and create stress (for you and possibly your roommate). So, let's keep it real. Music is a distraction!

The biggest myth (or lie) I want to address in this section is: *"I can read this chapter sitting up in my bed!"* Please, we all know the drill on this one! You start in an upright position in your bed. However, minutes later, your bed puts your brain into a "sleep mode" and you scoot down to a more comfortable position.

Why does this happen? Because your bed is the same place you sleep at the same time. So, your brain and body are sending the following messages back and forth:

"We are in bed now…
We sleep here…consistently…
We are getting sleepy…really sleepy…
You need a nap… Sleep induce now…"

Eventually, you have the book flat on the bed while propping your head up with your hand. That is what we called a PDP: "pre-drooling position." You are about to drool all over the textbook that cost too much money!

**STAY OUT OF BED WHEN STUDYING!**
It will work wonders for your productivity!

✦ ✦ ✦ ✦ ✦ ✦ ✦ ✦ ✦

## *Third thing about study:*
## No compromise!

✦ ✦ ✦ ✦ ✦ ✦ ✦ ✦ ✦

### What does "No compromise" mean?

**No Compromise means that you are on the A+ PLUS Plan and you study with other people who are on plan!** Here is a simple quiz: if you want to make A's, who should you study with? People who make A's! Who should you study with if you want to make B's? People who make B's! (We won't go any lower!) There is no compromise! **People who study together generally make the same grades.** If you want your A+ PLUS, don't do anything that hinders the new A+ PLUS way of learning.

**Sometimes, tough decisions may have to be made regarding your study group.** Let's say that you, John, and Christina formed an A+ PLUS study group. Three weeks later, John got discouraged. He said: "I don't want to do the A+ PLUS Plan anymore…too many BPs." At this juncture, you and Christina should encourage John as good friends would. Starting anything new can be difficult. It is perfectly normal and you should do your best to support John. However, if John keeps on complaining and is not making the effort to be on plan; it is time to "kick him to the curb!"

> If you don't know anyone who is on the A+ PLUS Plan at your school, you can either "be an army of one," encourage your friends to read this book or you can teach them the plan. (However, if you give them the $100 guarantee, it is on you!)

The principle is this: "If someone who you are studying with decides to not follow the plan, leave him or her alone <u>during</u> study time." All three of you can still hang out, go to the movies and have fun. Nevertheless, you and Christina should make it absolutely clear that John can't be a part of the study group, unless he is willing to get back on the A+ PLUS Plan! **The big idea here is to focus on purpose.** If John refuses to honor the purpose of the study group—getting an A+ PLUS, he doesn't fit into Christina's and your academic plan.

### No Compromise = Focus on Purpose

Remember, one thing always leads to another. Those students who compromise on "little things" (such as TOH) will soon find out that they have compromised the bigger picture of their academic success!

## Section Review—3.4

- **BP Notebook**
  - 1 BP Notebook organize all BPs (BPR, BPN, BPC)
  - Only bullet points in BP notebook
  - Take it everywhere
  - Review repetitiously

- **3 things about the word "study"**
  - Same time & place
  - Quiet place
  - No compromise

1. **Same Time & Place**
   - Prayer chair
   - Pre-conditioning saves time
   - 5-10 minutes to productive studying

2. **Quiet Place**
   - Individual situation
   - No TV, music
   - No studying in bed

3. **No Compromise**
   - Stay on plan
   - Study with others on plan
   - Focus on purpose: A+PLUS

## Guaranteed A+ PLUS Practice

- Put together your BP notebook
- Identify the same time and place that is conducive to study for you

My Conducive Place to Study: _____

- Identify 2-4 people that could be part of your A+ PLUS study group

| Day of week* | My same time to study |
|---|---|
| Monday | |
| Tuesday | |
| Wednesday | |
| Thursday | |
| Friday | |
| Saturday | |
| Sunday | |

*Please notice that we are not saying you have to study 7 days a week. We just want you to fill out the time on the days you actually will be studying.

## Chapter IV

# *Final Declaration*

Make a promise to yourself, and I want you to say this out loud: **I Promise to never, ever, ever STUDY AGAIN!** Are you in shock yet? Why in the world do I want you to promise NEVER to study again? After all, isn't this the Guaranteed A+ PLUS Learning System?

Here is the reality of the situation. The word "study" is simply too vague. Before the Guaranteed A+ PLUS plan, students would tell me that they studied all day long; but, it only meant they had a book open somewhere in their

> **I Promise to never, ever, ever STUDY AGAIN!**

rooms. They may have been on the phone talking about how much work they had to do, watching TV, surfing on the net or taking a nap. That is the type of "study" that does not produce the results we want.

To be on the A+ PLUS plan, I want you to strike the word "STUDY" from your vocabulary from now on!

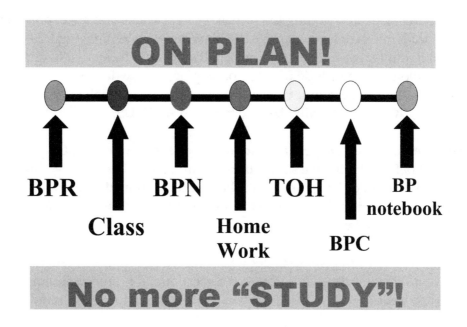

---

85

We are going to use our new concrete language: BPR, Class, BPN, HW, TOH, BPC and BP Notebook. These seven terms will replace the word study. Our "on-plan-ness" is easy to measure using this system. Just ask yourself the following questions:

1. Did I BPR at least 1-7 days before class?
2. Did I go to class and arrive 2 minutes early?
3. Did I BPN immediately after each class lecture or school?
4. Did I start the HW the day it was assigned?
5. Did I visit TOH this week for every class?
6. Did I BPC my returned HW and exams?
7. Did I take my BP notebook everywhere?

Here you have it—7 easy questions. It's simple to stay on plan and get a Guaranteed A+ PLUS!

I have what I call the "5 questions of life" and I always share them at the end of every seminar.

✦ ✦ ✦ ✦ ✦ ✦ ✦ ✦ ✦

## Donna O.'s 5 Questions of Life

- What do you want?
- What are the challenges you will face?
- How can you meet those challenges?
- What do you have to give up to get what you want?
- Is it worth it?

✦ ✦ ✦ ✦ ✦ ✦ ✦ ✦ ✦

By reading this book and putting the principles in practice, you are expressing the desire for academic excellence—an A+ PLUS no less! While pursuing this goal, there is no doubt that you may face some challenges—both external and internal. External challenges can include friends not on plan, family demands, and teachers that are difficult to understand. However, the most difficult challenges are the internal ones: "Can I do it? Will I be able to get an A+ PLUS?"

**You can meet and overcome every academic challenge by staying ON PLAN!** As I mentioned before, it will take some effort to start something new. I strongly believe everyone can do the plan. I am asking you to follow the Guaranteed A+ PLUS plan for at least 21 days to break any old/bad study habits and form the new positive habit of being ON PLAN!

So, what do you have to give up to get what you want? (We don't generally like this question.) It is not sleep. It is not even a social life. The answer is simple: give up the old concept of STUDYING! Are you going to give up the old mindset of "studying?" Are you willing to get off of the cycle of mediocrity and get into a proven system of success? If you are willing, get ON PLAN! Is it worth it? I guarantee that you will be pleased with your decision to stay ON PLAN!

One of my favorite inspiring sayings is a biblical scripture: "Therefore, if any person is in Christ, he is a new creation; the old has passed away, the new has come" (2 Corinthians 5:7). I use this scripture as an analogy for the Guaranteed A+ PLUS students at the end of every seminar.

**If you follow the Guaranteed A+ PLUS plan,
You are a new student and
that old student with average grades
no longer exists.**

**You are now a new student
on plan making easy A's because you are learning.
It does not matter where you are coming from academically,
it only matters where you want to go!
BE ON PLAN!**

# Part 2

# Applying the A+ PLUS Plan — A Student's Perspective

## By Y.C. Chen

I would like to dedicate this section to my parents. They cultivated in me a strong desire to learn and taught me to value education both in and out of the classroom. Most amazingly, they continue to be my No. 1 fans even though we are separated by the Pacific Ocean!

# Introduction to Part 2

* * * * * ✦ ✦ ✦ ✦ ✦ ✦ ✦ ✦ * * * *

Welcome to Part 2 of the Guaranteed A+ PLUS Plan. We specifically wrote this section to answer real-life questions and to address common situations high school students face everyday. In the past several years, we have literally answered thousands of questions posted by high school students from all over the country. There are many similar concerns, such as essay writing, test anxiety and SAT/ACT prep. Therefore, we selected the top 20 issues in order to compile this list of Frequently Asked Questions (FAQ). As you may have noticed, we also included answers to other questions in the form of "A+ PLUS Power Tips" in Part 1.

The FAQ list is meant to serve as a quick reference. My goal is to make it easy for you to use the Guaranteed A+ PLUS principles effectively. As I answer these FAQ, you will see how easy it is to use the A+ PLUS plan. I sincerely hope this part will continue to de-mystified learning and encourage you to stay ON PLAN!

Y.C. Chen

# Frequently Asked Questions (FAQ)

* * * ✦ ✦ ✦ ✦ ✦ ✦ ✦ ✦ ✦ ✦ * * *

**FAQ #1** Does this plan only work for smart students?

**FAQ #2** The teacher gives us his lecture notes or power point slides. Do I still have to BPR, take notes and BPN?

**FAQ #3** When should I BPN if I have sports or work right after school?

**FAQ #4** It takes me longer to read with BPR; what should I do?

**FAQ #5** How does the principle of "starting the HW the day it is assigned" apply to a term paper?

**FAQ #6** How can BPs help me write an essay?

**FAQ #7** How can BPs help me with a foreign language class?

**FAQ #8** Can you show me how to use BPs for multi-step math/science problems?

**FAQ #9** How can the A+ PLUS Plan help me with ACT/SAT (or other standardized test) preparation?

**FAQ #10** When should I study for an exam?

**FAQ #11** How do I deal with test anxiety?

**FAQ #12** What are some test-taking strategies BEFORE the exam?

**FAQ #13** What are some test-taking strategies DURING the exam?

**FAQ #14** What are some test-taking strategies AFTER the exam?

**FAQ #15** How do I make my bed in 3 seconds or less?

**FAQ #16** How can I keep my room clean?

**FAQ #17** How do I manage my time on the Guaranteed A+ PLUS plan?

**FAQ #18** How do I catch up without falling behind?

**FAQ #19** I just learned the A+ PLUS Plan and I have a test this week; what can I do?

**FAQ #20** If I have questions after reading this book, who can help me?

## *Frequently Asked Questions*

### FAQ #1   Does this plan only work for smart students?

Many students take one look at my Chinese face and assume that I am smart! Or they assume I am good at math and I can do all that stuff seen in a bad Kung-Fu movie. Let me help you out—forget all those stereotypes! I did not learn English until the 7th grade. So, I actually had challenges beyond course content. If the Guaranteed A+ PLUS plan worked for me, it will definitely work for you!

**The A+ PLUS Plan works because it taught me how to learn!** It uses brain-based learning strategies. The Bullet Point system helps you put information in a format that your brain can process quicker. It is also easier for you to remember. That means you can use more of your brain's power to learn more effectively.

If you still think my story is unique, allow me to share one more success story. Kevin is a high school student from New York. He was having a really difficult time with Biology and had failed 2 tests. By using the techniques from the A+ PLUS Plan, he became motivated to learn. After spending some time on BPR, BPN, BPC as well as going to TOH to get more help, he scored an 85 on the next test and passed the class with a B+! All within 6 weeks!

### FAQ #2   The teacher gives us his lecture notes or power point slides. Do I still have to BPR, take notes and BPN?

As more high schools become equipped with the latest technology, it is not uncommon for teachers to distribute their lecture material using power point slides or handouts prior to class. However, when students rely solely on the given outline, they often become passive listeners and miss critical information from the lecture! It may be convenient to refer to the teacher's outline but **it is not a replacement for your BPR, class notes or BPN.**

During lectures, teachers often cover more information than included on the out-line and show various examples. Sometimes they will purposely or accidentally drop hints regarding the test material. However, if you did not BPR beforehand, you may not be able to benefit from these hints since you are listening to the information for the first time.

Taking notes during a lecture also allows you to benefit from these important additional details! If you wish, you can take notes directly on the printed presen-tation or lecture outline. In addition, BPN offers a quick and concise way to cap-ture all the knowledge you learned during class. It will check your understanding and make doing the HW much faster and easier.

## FAQ #3   When should I BPN if I work or have practice right after school?

BPN is typically done immediately after a class lecture or after school. If you are not able to BPN immediately after your class lecture (during the designated homework time before the bell rings), please <u>do not BPN</u> during your next class. (Unfortunately, some students have tried this.)

Based on our experience, most work schedules can be "re-scheduled" to give you an extra 25-30 minutes of BPN time prior to work. Again, we are not asking you to rewrite your entire class notes, only to summarize the important concepts. It will only take 25-30 minutes for 5 to 6 academic classes.

As far as practice, coaches are generally very supportive of your schoolwork and interested in keeping you eligible for the team. Politely ask them if you can do your BPN before practice. Many of them will happily agree. (We had a student who is a track and field star. She did her BPN right on the bleacher prior to warm-up jogs.)

For some major team sports such as football, the arrangement may not be possible. Your next option is to do BPN as soon as the practice is over before hanging out with friends, getting something to eat or turning on the TV. Remember, there are 2.5 million dollars at stake here for YOU!

## FAQ #4   It takes me longer to read with BPR; what should I do?

Anytime we learn to use a new tool, it always seems to take longer than before to perform a similar task. In actuality, BPR may take longer in the beginning. With minimal practice, however, the BPR process can be easily mastered and it will actually save you a lot of time in the long run.

**One mistake students often make is writing down too much information in their BPR.** Remember, only do BPR on important (or testable) information. You can always show your BPR to your teacher and ask if you are summarizing the relevant information.

One student had a history teacher who reviewed his BPs and told him what she considered to be important. **Remember, BPs are not complete sentences.** (This is slightly counter-intuitive to years of English classes.) Keeping BPs less than 5 words allows your brain to process and store the information much better and faster.

In short, BPR is the foundation of the Guaranteed A+ PLUS Learning System. If you BPR properly, you can expect at least a B average! But, follow all 3 steps and you'll get your A+ PLUS.

### FAQ #5   How does the principle of "starting the HW the day it is assigned" apply to a term paper?

The average high school student panics when he or she realizes that there are only 2 days left before the term paper, which was assigned 4 weeks prior, is due. The procrastinating mentality of "I can do it later" has been exercised. Seriously, when was the last time that "later" ever came?

The same principle of starting your homework the day it is assigned applies here as well. For example, if you have to do a term paper, you can still start the term paper the day it is assigned. You can do one of the following things:

1. **BP the instructions and suggestions from the teacher**
2. **Start a list of potential topics**
3. **Identify possible resources**
4. **BP any initial ideas/thoughts**
5. **Put together a plan with a timeline**

It is very important to BP and follow your teacher's instructions. You don't want to lose points on technicalities. For example, some teachers require students to follow a specific citation format for references.

In addition, the day the term paper is assigned, students often have ideas that are forgotten by the time they actually sit down to write the paper. Keeping a list of potential topics will solve that problem.

By the way, never start writing a term paper unless you have checked your topic with the teacher. The teacher can help you clarify the topic and give you additional input that would be helpful. One of our students once finished 50% of an essay without discussing it with the teacher first. Imagine the horror when he found out that he had misinterpreted the essay topic and had to start over. It was very stressful! A quick conversation with the teacher would have helped him avoid all the un-necessary drama!

### FAQ #6   How can BPs help me write an essay?

The Guaranteed A+ PLUS essay strategy is simple and can save you considerable time. Essays are normally written about something you were required to read. In high school, the instructor typically will share the essay topic with students prior to assigning the required reading. **Your first step is to do focused bullet points (BPs) on the book or article that you are reading. Focused BPs are from selected parts of the reading that you may want to write about.**

By keeping the paper topics or goals of the reading in the back of your mind, you only have to BP the relevant information that you will consider including in your paper. You don't need an outline of the entire book with every detail or fact. You are basically **focusing** your reading to look for and do BPs only on things that may help in the essay-writing process.

After the reading is complete, **the next step is to brainstorm with BPs**. This is where BPs will help your creative juices to flow with ease. While you brainstorm, you can use BPs to document various ideas from different sections of the reading materials, class notes, discussions with your teacher or classmates, etc. You can do this either with paper or directly in a word-processing program. Personally, I prefer paper because I enjoy the freedom to doodle and draw as I think. Don't worry about grammar or references at this point, just focus on putting down your ideas in BP format. Remember, a BP has 3-5 words.

**The third step is to structure the essay with BPs**. When you review your BPs from the brainstorming sessions, you will easily discover some BPs have related ideas. Begin by clustering BPs with similar ideas or themes. Then write a sentence from each bullet point in the cluster. Or simply take each BP and write a sentence with it in your own words, without clustering. You will put related sentences together into paragraphs in the next step. **Either way works!** The process is flexible and you can decide what is best for you. The third step is also very helpful if your teacher requires you to turn in an outline prior to writing the actual essay.

**The last step is to formulate different paragraphs and the essay.** After turning your BPs into sentences, you simply arrange them into paragraphs that make sense. Don't worry if the paragraphs seem disjointed. As you reorder the paragraphs into an essay, you will begin to write the necessary transitions to make it a cohesive paper with an introduction and conclusion.

**The essay-writing process is now made simple because you have a step-by-step plan that helps you from start to finish**. In addition, you have documented and clarified your ideas with BPs, sentences and paragraphs. You will never waste time just staring at a blank computer screen again!

✦ ✦ ✦ ✦ ✦ ✦ ✦ ✦ ✦

## *Writing Essay with BPs*

1. **Do focused BPR on reading material**
2. **Brainstorm with BPs**
3. **Structure essay BPs into sentences**
4. **Formulate paragraphs → paper**

✦ ✦ ✦ ✦ ✦ ✦ ✦ ✦ ✦

## Please allow the simplified example below to illustrate the procedure.

### Assigned Reading:

*Fish is Fish* (Lionni, 1970) describes a fish that is keenly interested in learning about what happens on the land, but the fish cannot explore land because it can only breathe in water. It befriends a tadpole that grows into a frog and eventually goes out onto the land. The frog returns to the pond a few weeks later and reports on what he has seen. The frog describes all kinds of things like birds, cows and people. The book shows pictures of the fish's representations of each of these descriptions: each is a fish-like form that is slightly adapted to accommodate the frog's descriptions. For example, people are imagined to be fish that walk on their tailfins, birds are fish with wings, cows are fish with udders. The tale illustrates both the creative opportunities and dangers inherent in the fact that people construct new knowledge based on their current knowledge.

*Fish Is Fish* is relevant not only for young children, but for learners of all ages. For example, college students often have developed beliefs about physical and biological phenomena that fit their experiences, but do not fit scientific accounts of these phenomena. These misconceptions must be addressed in order for them to change their beliefs.

## Essay Topic

In the Guaranteed A+ PLUS book, the authors urge the readers to let go of the old concept of "studying." Based on the information given above, explain in 2-3 paragraphs the importance of giving up the old mindset of "Studying" while being "On Plan."

## 1) Do focused BPR on Reading Material

| |
|---|
| •Fish is fish (Lionni) |
| • Fish befriends tadpole → frog |
| • Returns from land, describes experience |
| |
| • Fish's interpretation of frog's description |
| • Everything → all fish like |
| • People = Fish walking on tailfins |
| • Birds = Fish w/wings |
| • Cows = Fish w/udders |
| |
| • Principle → opportunities & dangers |
| • Constructing new knowledge on current understanding |
| |
| • Relevancies: learners, all ages |
| • Example: College students |
| • Hold beliefs - physical & biological phenomena |
| • Fit personal experiences, not scientific facts |
| • Addressing misconceptions: change student's beliefs |

## 2) Brainstorm with BPs

Students organize their ideas in different ways. Below is an example of my brainstorming session. I wrote down several ideas as they came to mind in BP format. Then, I grouped similar ideas using arrows and circled the idea chosen for the thesis statement.

- Relating <u>Fish</u> to 4.0 = How?

- From book: Give up "study"

- Study—Too general / fuzzy

- 3 things about STUDY
    1. Consistent time / place
    2. Conducive
    3. No compromise

- 5 questions of life
    - see book for questions

- Give up <u>old mind set</u>— "studying"
    - Give up old ways of thinking
    - Become new students

- A++ / On-Plan things
    - bpr, class, bpn, hw, poh
    - BPC & BP notebook
    - DOJ: "concrete & measurable"

- **A++ → Address misconceptions of "study"**
    Change my belief on study

- Article: fish-like people (?)

- Theme: Building new on old knowledge

    - Creative yet dangerous
    - Why? Misinterpretations

- Old mind set
    → study / old knowledge

- A++ plan: new knowledge
    - link? New knowledge fish gained.
    - ANSWER TO ESSAY / THESIS!

- Getting new knowledge (A++ plan)
    - Different from old plan
    - or Non-existing study plan!

Danger: based new knowledge / A++
    - on old knowledge / study

- **Why?**
    - **Misinterpretations?**
    - **Not following the plan?**
    - **Not learn as much?**
    - **Learn the wrong thing !!!**
        - **Is that possible?**

- MY LINK: old vs new
    - Build new on old
    - Ex: A++ on old mindset

- Problem: learn the wrong thing
    - or not learn as much
    - not as effective in learning

### 3) Structure Essay: BPs into Sentences

### 4) Formulate paragraphs → paper

The writing process is as individualized as it is creative. Therefore, we won't actually write the whole essay for this exercise. If you understand the principles and examples shown in Step 1 and 2, you are well on your way to a great essay!

### FAQ #7 How can BPs help me with a foreign language class?

The process of learning a foreign language is identical to how you learned English or your native language. The problem is that most of us have forgotten how because it occurred so long ago. When used correctly, BPs are really helpful because they help to prepare your brain toward learning another language. For the purpose of this illustration, let's assume this student is taking Spanish.

## Vocabulary

The basic building block of any language is its vocabulary. To best remember vocabulary, you write the Spanish word first and write the English definition as a sub BP. We also suggest that you write a short (3-5 word) sentence using the new vocabulary word.

| Vocabulary – Lesson 1 |
| --- |
| Buenos días |
| • Good morning |
| • Buenos días senor' Chavis. |
| |
| Buenos tardes |
| • Good afternoon |
| |
| Buenos noches |
| • Good evening |

## Short Phrases / Q & A

BPs for short phrases follow the same basic format of the vocabulary with Spanish first and the English translation second. In Spanish, there is a differentiation between informal and formal tones of the language. This student includes the formal and informal information as part of the sub BP.

| ¡Hola! ¿Que tal? |
| --- |
| • Hi. How are things? (informal) |
| |
| ¿Cómo está / estás? |
| • How are you? (formal) |

| ¿Como se llama? |
| --- |
| Me llamo José |
| • (literally) How are you called? |
| • I am called José |
| |
| ¿Cual es su nombre? |
| Mi nombre es José |
| • What is your name? |
| • My name es José |

As you create BPs for a foreign language and review these BPs repeatedly, you should say these words out loud. This will help your pronunciation and transition them from short-term to long-term memory quicker.

## Grammar

Grammar is perhaps the most confusing part of a foreign language for most beginners. (Let's face it, even for native speakers, English grammar can still be a very illusive concept.) It seems like every time we learn a grammar rule, there are also some exceptions to that rule that we have to learn! The idea here is to use BPs to learn the general rules as well as the exceptions.

> **By reviewing BPs repeatedly and saying them out loud, your brain will get used to the idea of different verb tenses and pronouns faster than you can imagine!**

### BPs Examples on Personal Pronouns
*For this student - (m) indicates masculine form, (f) feminine

| yo |
| --- |
| • I |
| |
| nosotros (m) |
| nosotras (f) |
| • We |
| |
| tú (informal) |
| Usted (formal) |
| • You |
| |
| vosotros (m) |
| vosotras (f) |
| • you all |

### BPs Example on conjugating - AR verbs in Spanish

| Hablar (to speak) |
| --- |
| • Yo hablo |
| • Tú hablas |
| • él, ella, Usted habla |
| • ellos, ellas, Ustedes hablan |
| • nosotros hablamos |
| • vosotros habláis |

These are some basic BPs for your foreign language class. Once armed with these simple tools, you will be ready to tackle the more complex sentence structures and grammar rules in advanced levels of foreign language classes.

## FAQ #8  Can you show me how to use BPs for multi-step math/science problems?

In part 1 of this book, we explained the A+ PLUS system for doing BPs for a formula. It can be even more beneficial if you use BPs to unlock the secrets of multi-step math/science problems.

### Sample Math Text: Median

The median is another measure of central location for data. The median is the value in the middle when the data items are arranged in ascending order (rank ordered from smallest to largest). If there are an odd number of items, the median is the value of the middle item. If there is an even number of items, there is no single middle item. In this case, we define the median to be the average of the values for the middle two items.

#### Example BP (Student A)

Median: Middle value
- Rank order, smallest to largest
- Odd # ➔ middle value
- Even # ➔ average, 2 middle #

#### Example BP (Student B)

Median: put no. small ➔ big
- Odd data no.
  - Median = Middle value
- Even data no.
  - Median = average 2 middle no.

By doing BPs on the procedures used to calculate median, both students now have the exact steps to correctly solve for median every time!

## FAQ #9  How can the A+ PLUS Plan help me with ACT/SAT (or other standardized test) preparation?

There are many ACT and SAT preparation programs. There are books, computer programs and even classes available for just about every budget. Guaranteed A+ PLUS is not designed to replace these programs. We specialize in helping you to get the most out of these programs.

We hear this horror story all the time. Parents paid lots of money for their child to enroll in one of the expensive programs. However, the student did not really learn the material, and most often forgot the material they did learn, one month after the program. Just think about all that wasted money!

**BPC is your best friend for standardized test preparation.** Most test prep programs offer tips and practice tests. Students will take a practice test, get a score and put it aside. They are actually missing the biggest benefit! By doing BPC, you can test your understanding and make sure you understand the principles of what is being tested. While the test questions will never be the same, they are all written to test the same set of pre-defined principles. If you can do BPC on practice test problems, you are guaranteed a higher test score because you now know the principles.

Because every test is different, we offer additional information geared toward specific tests at www.NoMoreStudy.com.

## FAQ #10  When should I study for an exam?

Now for the big question—when should I study for my exams? **The answer is NEVER!** With Guaranteed A+ PLUS, you are systematically preparing for exams as you BPR, BPN, BPC, go to class, do HW and utilize TOH. The information you learned is being committed to your long-term memory through the review process. Before an exam there is no reason to cram or panic because you have actually already learned the material!

All that is left for you to do is review BPR, BPN and BPC in your BP notebook. You should also work extra problems for speed and accuracy. In a history class for example, it may be sufficient just to review bullet points from class. For the Algebra exam, you may want to work different problem types, in addition to reviewing bullet points. So seriously, no more all night study sessions! They are now a thing of the past!

## FAQ #11  How do I deal with test anxiety?

Test anxiety is a common issue among students. Students often report extreme nervousness, emotional roller coasters or the dreaded "blank-out" effect before and during exams. Test anxiety causes stress because it takes you away from giving 100% of yourself while prepping for and taking exams. Many times, students have adequately prepared for an exam, but that little nagging/worrying voice in the back of their minds actually sabotages their effort by causing test anxiety. On the Guaranteed A+ PLUS Plan, **test anxiety can be greatly reduced or even eliminated by doing 3 things:**

## 1) Enjoy your weekly stress relieving /preventing activity.

These activities are helpful because they prevent stress from building up to the point where it becomes anxiety. If possible, schedule a special session of your stress relieving/preventing activity the night prior to the exam. I usually set aside some time before an exam to sip on some coffee (decaf) and read a book. Often, I will read my Bible and remind myself that my GPA does not determine who I am. Sometimes, I will enjoy a great science fiction novel and let my imagination run wild. These activities usually give me an extra boost and allow my body and mind to relax.

## 2) Get 7-8 hours of uninterrupted sleep the night before.

On the A+ PLUS Plan, you are guaranteed 8 hours of sleep, even the night before an exam. So many horror stories about disastrous test performances start with the students doing an all-nighter the night before a critical exam. Would you trust someone to drive your brand new car when he or she was sleep deprived and delirious? Of course not! Walking into an exam half-asleep and physically exhausted is a sure-fire recipe for disaster.

## 3) Stay ON-PLAN!

When you are confident in your understanding of the class material, your stress level and test anxiety automatically reduces. The Guaranteed A+ PLUS plan makes it easy for you to remember the material. When you are on-plan, course materials are stored in your long-term memory by repetitious review of BPR, BPN, and BPC. In short, staying on-plan is your best defense against test anxiety. Before the exam, simply review your BPR, BPN and BPC to reinforce your learning. If it is a problem-based exam such as physics or math, do some practice problems to increase speed and accuracy. This will further increase your confidence as well.

+ + + + + + + + + +

### *Dealing with Test Anxiety*

1. **Enjoy your weekly stress relieving / preventing activity**
2. **Get 7-8 hours of uninterrupted sleep the night before**
3. **Stay ON-PLAN!**

+ + + + + + + + + +

## FAQ #12 What are some test-taking strategies BEFORE the exam?

## 1) Pack your bag the night before

Nothing is worse than walking into an exam only to realize that you forgot a tool needed to complete the exam. I have personally witnessed a case in which a student walked into an "OPEN BOOK" exam but left her book at home. She planned on borrowing one from the teacher but it was already loaned out to another student. As a result, she had to wait for someone to finish their exam before she could borrow the book to look up some formulas. This is unnecessary drama that could easily be avoided by preparing your book bag with all the necessary tools the night before the exam. This way, you won't forget what you need even if you are in a rush.

## 2) Avoid pre-exam chatters

When a student arrives early for an exam and starts talking to his anxious classmates (pre-exam chatters), his anxiety level can easily be increased and his confidence can easily be destroyed. He could actually perform poorly despite the fact that he is well prepared for the test.

Refuse to allow any negative or defeating thoughts into your head! You are ON-PLAN and more than adequately prepared for the exam because the information is stored in your long-term memory!

Someone in your class will always have the need to complain and be nervous. Some will even ask you if you are prepared. You can simply smile and tell them: "Yes, I am prepared because I am on the A+ PLUS PLAN!" Some students put their head on the table and rest until the instructor starts the class. If headphones are allowed in your school, you can simply listen to music until it is time for class.

✦ ✦ ✦ ✦ ✦ ✦ ✦ ✦ ✦

### *Prior to the Exam*

1. **Pack your bag the night before.**
2. **Avoid pre-exam chatters.**

✦ ✦ ✦ ✦ ✦ ✦ ✦ ✦ ✦

## FAQ #13 What are some test-taking strategies DURING the exam?

## 1) Check all instructions FIRST

We all know the importance of paying attention to both verbal and written instructions. Unfortunately, however, students often tend to jump into exams and immediately start to answer questions. A friend received a lower grade in an earth science class because he answered all 3 short-answer questions when the teacher only required him to answer 2. Because he had to allow time to write 3 answers, he did not have time to develop any of his answers fully. As soon as you get the test, take a minute to look through the instructions to know what is required of you.

## 2) Preview exam questions

We suggest that you preview the exam questions. As you preview, BPs will start pouring into your brain because the material is stored in your long-term memory. If time allows, you can quickly write down BPs on a sheet of scratch paper or the margin of the exam paper. Once this process is finished, you are well on your way to successfully completing your exam. Do not worry if you don't know how to approach a question. Answer the problems that you can do first. As you work through the exam, additional BPs will be triggered that will probably help you answer the other questions.

### Example for Problem-based Exams

A problem on a chemistry exam reads:

> **Suppose you have a gas with a 45.0 ml volume and a pressure of 760 mmHg. If the pressure is increased to 800mmHg and the temperature remains constant, what is the new volume?**

As you preview, here are some BPs that may have been triggered.

- T = constant ➜ **Boyle's law**
  - $P_1V_1 = P_2V_2$

Now, you have the equation to solve the problem and you can preview the next question.

### Example for Essay-based Exams

The paragraph in the essay exam reads:

> **Define and explain the third step of the Guaranteed A+ PLUS Learning System in the order in which it was presented.**

As you preview the question, here are some BPs that may have come into your mind.

- **Define & Explain ➜ 3rd step**
  - **IN ORDER**

  - **DO IT IN ORDER!**
    BPR
    Class
    BPN
    HW
    TOH

BPC
BP notebook

By doing BPs while previewing, you now have the general structure of the essay. You can continue to develop the outline by adding more BPs and then converting all BPs into sentences for your essay.

Notice that doing BPs helps you to make sure that all relevant issues are addressed: the essay has to be explained "in order." Missing important essay key-words such as "contrast" or "define and give an example" can really put a damper on your grades.

### 3) Finish the exam with confidence

I suggest you use a watch or the clock in the classroom (if it is accurate) to help you keep track of the time. All that is left for you to do is to complete the exam with confidence. You can be confident because:

1.  The material is in your long-term memory.
2.  You have previewed the exam questions.
3.  BPs give you a strategy for answering the questions.

✦ ✦ ✦ ✦ ✦ ✦ ✦ ✦ ✦

## *During the Exam*

### 1. CHECK all instructions FIRST
### 2. Preview all exam questions
### • Write BPs as you preview
### 3. Finish the exam with confidence

✦ ✦ ✦ ✦ ✦ ✦ ✦ ✦ ✦

**FAQ #14    What are some test-taking strategies AFTER the exam?**

### 1) Don't compare answers

We all know the familiar scene: students huddle together after the exam and com-pare answers. To be honest, there are times my curiosity got the best of me and I compared answers with my classmates. I soon realized, however, that it was a lose-lose situation. Even when my answer matched that of a classmate, there was still a strong possibility that we BOTH HAD IT WRONG! If my answer did not match, I spent the next couple of days consumed by stress! I learned my lesson the hard way!

In reality, comparing answers after an exam is both unproductive and stress-inducing! It is unproductive because without going to the source (teacher), you never really know if your answers are correct. Your time is not being used productively. It is stress-inducing because the test is over and there is really nothing you can do about it. If your classmates want to compare answers with you after a test, just politely let them know that you are happy that the test is over and that you want to move on to your next class.

## 2) BPC returned exams

## 3) TOH

Since the benefits of doing BPC and utilizing TOH have been explained in previous chapters, I won't repeat those points here. I will however share a real story with you that I believe will solidify the benefits in your mind.

Melanie took a world geography class during her sophomore year. She made a low B on the midterm while half of her classmates got C's and D's! As a student on the A+ PLUS Plan, Melanie was very discouraged.

Nevertheless, she stayed on plan by doing her BPCs on that midterm and utilizing TOH to receive additional help. One week later, the teacher gave everyone a chance to replace the midterm grade by taking another test. In fact, the teacher actually gave the class the exact same test that they took at midterm! Armed with knowledge from BPC and TOH, Melanie aced that exam! However, much to her teacher's dismay, the majority of her classmates (who were not ON PLAN) did not improve their grades and some even had lower scores!

✦ ✦ ✦ ✦ ✦ ✦ ✦ ✦ ✦ ✦

### *After the Exam*

1. **Don't compare answers**
2. **BPC returned exams**
3. **TOH**

✦ ✦ ✦ ✦ ✦ ✦ ✦ ✦ ✦ ✦

### FAQ #15 How do I make my bed in 3 seconds or less?

Let's face it, making up your bed every morning is a chore that is enjoyed by few. For some of us, our beds are in a permanent state of disarray with the bed sheets, comforter, pillows and some school-related papers all in one gigantic clump. The good news is it doesn't have to be this way anymore! As promised in Part 1 of the book, I will show you how to make your bed so that it only takes 3 seconds or less to remake it each morning. You don't even have to sleep on top of the comforter!

This technique is referred to as "hospital corners" or "military corners." Here are the steps toward making a perfect "corner":

1) Put a fitted sheet on your mattress first.

2) Place the flat sheet on the bed. Tuck it in at the end of the bed where your feet will be. Do not tuck the sides!

3) On one side, about 1 foot from the end of the bed, lift the bottom of the hanging sheet and place it on the bed. Lift it up so it makes a diagonal fold (about a 45 degree angle).

4) Take the part of the sheet that is still hanging in that spot and tuck it under the mattress. Drop the fold and pull it until the sheet is smooth. This creates a double-tuck. Do the same procedure on the other side.

5) Simply pull the flat sheet to cover the rest of the bed. The flat sheet can be folded down at the top. If you use a blanket, do the corners the same way. Now add a comforter. Put a pillow on top of the bed, and you are done.

Because the flat sheet is folded in a double tuck, it won't get pulled off of the bed when you toss and turn at night (no matter how badly you sleep). In the morning,

all you have to do is straighten out the top sheet, pull up your comforter or blanket and reposition your pillows or other cute stuffed animals (if you have any). That generally takes only 3 seconds. Now you can have a cleaner room in just 3 seconds every morning!

### FAQ #16    How do I keep my room clean?

The objective here is to never let your room get dirty. As Donna O. mentioned, there are 3 main reasons that your room could be dirty. Since we already discussed the express "bed-making" techniques in FAQ #15, we will concentrate on dealing with piles of clothes (dirty or clean) in your room.

To get rid of piles of clothes, purchase 2 upright rectangular hampers with lids. (They can be easily found in your neighborhood Wal-Mart or Target and cost about $5 each.) Use one hamper to store light-colored laundry and the other one for dark-colored clothes. When you get undressed, immediately place the dirty laundry into its "rightful resting place." **By doing this, the piles of clothes are eliminated, and your laundry is already separated.** If you plan to wear something again, (students generally wear the same jeans at least 3 times as a rule of thumb!), go ahead and hang

it up. It only takes 5 seconds to hang up a pair of jeans. It takes about 10 seconds to justify adding it to your ever-growing pile of clothes!

It is also very simple to manage those piles of paper in your room. If the paper is school related, it belongs in one of your regular class notebooks or BP notebook. If the paper is not school related, use a desktop sorter to put the papers into different categories. Some common categories are:

- College application related
- Extra-curricular related
- Friends
- Upcoming events

Having a clean room is easier than you think. **The principle is this: everything has a place and everything is in its place.** You will be able to find things more quickly and avoid disorderly surroundings that can hinder your grades.

## FAQ #17  How do I manage my time on the Guaranteed A+ PLUS plan?

As we discussed in Part 1, your schedule is fairly routine in high school. If you are "On Plan" as a high school student, you simply do BPN at the end of the school day or at the end of class if your teacher gives you time. You also start on HW and BPR when you get home and probably finish up after dinner. Remember, when you are "On Plan" as a high school student, you only 'study" 11 hours per week instead of 22 hours compared to other college-bound students.

However, there is still a need to create a schedule that guides your entire week. So, you no longer have to wonder: "What am I supposed to be doing now?" We will take you through filling out your own schedule step-by-step. From now on, you should refer to your schedule as your "Plan for Success!"

## Step 1: Schedule Non-negotiable Items

**We have included two sample schedules and blank forms for your use in the Appendix section.** If you want to, you can also set up an Excel spreadsheet and prepare your schedule that way.

Non-negotiable items are those that cannot be moved around or skipped in your pursuit of an A+ PLUS.

A. **Pencil in the exact time for each of your classes**
   - Use the subject name, such as English. **Do not** write "class."

B. **Determine a realistic time that you need to get up and prepare for class**
   - Calculate the time that you need to go to bed the previous night in order to get at least 7-8 hours of uninterrupted sleep.

C. **Plan time for Personal Hygiene (PH)**
   - You know what you need to do.

D. **Schedule your Bullet Point Notes (BPNs)**
   - Write it as BPN-Class Name. For example: BPN-English.
   - Plan 5 to 10 minutes for BPNs for <u>each</u> hour of class.
   - Schedule them either at the end of a class lecture or end of a school day.

E. **Write in each of your Teacher's Office Hours (TOH)**
   - Write it as TOH-Class Name. For example: TOH-Math.
   - Plan to spend approximately 15 to 20 minutes for each TOH.
   - You can easily schedule 1 TOH per day for each of your classes.

F. **Write in your Homework (HW) time**
   - Write it as HW-Class Name. For example: HW-Biology.
   - Start all HW the day it is assigned.
   - Start with your hardest class first.

G. **Schedule Bullet Point Reading (BPR)**
   - Write it as BPR-Class Name. For example: BPR-History.
   - Schedule your BPR at least **1 day before class**.

H. **Schedule Bullet Point Concepts (BPC)**
   - Write it as BPC-Class Name. For example: BPC-Math.
   - Depending on your teachers, BPCs can be scheduled the day HW is returned or once a week for all classes.
   - BPCs normally require 10 to 15 minutes for a standard HW set.

I. **Set aside time for planning**
   - Take 15 to 30 minutes per week to schedule negotiable activities.

J. **Take time to relax**
   - Schedule breaks each day.
   - Allow 1 to 2 hours a week for your stress relieving/preventing activity.

K. **Schedule time for Church/Worship**
   - For those who attend, this is considered a non-negotiable activity because you can't call your pastor or leader and ask him to reschedule service for you.

L. **Highlight all non-negotiable items on your schedule**
   - This is the only use you will have for your highlighter under the Guaranteed A+ PLUS plan.

## Step 2: Schedule Negotiable Items

Negotiable items are those that can be moved around or skipped entirely if necessary in your pursuit of an A+ PLUS. However, be diligent to schedule these realis-
tically. Negotiable items can fit into any of the blank spaces still existing on the
schedule.

   M.  **Schedule work hours (your second job) if necessary**
- Work is typically considered negotiable because
    1. Your work schedule can often be changed to fit your new schedule.
    2. If you need to spend time doing BPR, BPN, HW, TOH and BPC,
       work can often be rescheduled or shortened temporarily.
    3. Most employers allow students to work flexible hours.

   N.  **Schedule other negotiable items. These can include:**
- Meals
- Exercise
- Laundry/Cleaning
- Social time
- Extra-curricular Activities

| Class: | Class: | Class: | Class: | Class: |
|---|---|---|---|---|
| ❏ BPR<br>❏ CLASS<br>❏ BPN<br>❏ HW<br>❏ TOH<br>❏ BPC | ❏ BPR<br>❏ CLASS<br>❏ BPN<br>❏ HW<br>❏ TOH<br>❏ BPC | ❏ BPR<br>❏ CLASS<br>❏ BPN<br>❏ HW<br>❏ TOH<br>❏ BPC | ❏ BPR<br>❏ CLASS<br>❏ BPN<br>❏ HW<br>❏ TOH<br>❏ BPC | ❏ BPR<br>❏ CLASS<br>❏ BPN<br>❏ HW<br>❏ TOH<br>❏ BPC |

- Errands
- Hobbies
- Anything else…

## Step 3: Reality Check – "Keep it real!"

   O.  **Are you operating in reality?**
- Did you schedule BPR or HW on a Friday night?
- Depending on your preference, sometimes it is not realistic to schedule
  BPR or HW on a Saturday morning!

   P.  **Did you forget anything?**
- Use the following chart to determine if your schedule has all of the "bare
  necessities" for each class:

## FAQ #18 How do I catch up without falling behind?

Let's just say that you began the Guaranteed A+ PLUS Plan after the beginning of your current semester. You want to stay on plan, but you already have a backlog of reading and homework. We will teach you how to get caught up without falling behind by showing you how to take advantage of the "negotiable" time in your schedule.

In short, we will quickly walk you through the process of identifying those tasks that need to be performed (using your new terminology: BPR, BPN, BPC, HW) and deciding when to do them. The secret to not getting further behind is in sticking with your non-negotiable activities as illustrated in your schedule.

By doing this, most students get caught up within a week. Of course, this all depends on how much you want to sacrifice in terms of negotiable activities, such as errands or social time. There will be a cost, but there will also be great benefits!

## STEP ONE: Breaking it Down

Now you will separate your backlog of work using your new "On Plan" terms. List one chapter of BPR or one HW assignment or one week of BPNs or one Exam/HW worth of BPCs that you need to catch up with on each blank line. For example, if you need to BPR and HW chapters 4 and 5 in English along with BPN and BPC for Math, put these tasks on separate lines.

> **Preparation: At this point, you should have already completed the weekly schedule. If not, see FAQ #17 for detailed instructions! DO NOT attempt to do the following exercise without first finishing your A+ PLUS "Plan for Success"!**

**EXAMPLE**

It is very important to list individual activities or assignments.

### "Catching up without falling behind" Planner - Page 1

| Class | Activity | Chapter or Assignment | ... | ... | ... |
|---|---|---|---|---|---|
| Eng | BPR | Chap 4 | | | |
| Eng | BPR | Chap 5 | | | |
| Eng | HW | Chap 4 | | | |
| Eng | HW | Chap 5 | | | |
| Math | BPN | This week | | | |
| Math | BPN | Last week | | | |
| Math | BPC | Quiz #2 | | | |
| Math | BPC | Test 1 | | | |

Notice:
- You do not need to do BPR for all missed reading if you are drastically behind, unless you know for a fact that you need details from the text.
- Blank A+ PLUS Planner pages can be found in the Appendix.

## STEP TWO: Estimating Time

For each line entered, estimate the amount of time you feel it will take you to complete the task. For instance, you may decide that it will take you one hour to BPR Chapter 4 for your English class. Write this in the column, **Estimated Time**.

| Class | Activity | Chapter or Assignment | Estimated Time | ... | ... |
|---|---|---|---|---|---|
| Eng | BPR | Chap 4 | 1 Hour | | |
| Eng | BPR | Chap 5 | 1 Hour | | |
| Eng | HW | Chap 4 | 1.5 Hour | | |
| Eng | HW | Chap 5 | 1.5 Hour | | |
| Math | BPN | This week | 15 Min. | | |
| Math | BPN | Last week | 15 Min. | | |
| Math | BPC | Quiz #2 | 30 Min. | | |
| Math | BPC | Text 1 | 45 Min. | | |

## STEP THREE: "Keeping it REAL!"

Determine your own personal **Human Factor**. This is the amount of time you need to add to your estimation to get closer to reality. If projects tend to take you longer than you anticipate, you may have a Human Factor of 30 minutes or even more. If you always complete your projects in the amount of time you estimate, you can use a Human Factor of 0 minutes. Write the number in the **Human Factor** column.

| Class | Activity | Chapter or Assignment | Estimated Time | Human Factor | ... |
|---|---|---|---|---|---|
| Eng | BPR | Chap 4 | 1 Hour | 30 Min. | |
| Eng | BPR | Chap 5 | 1 Hour | 30 Min. | |
| Eng | HW | Chap 4 | 1.5 Hour | 0 Min. | |
| Eng | HW | Chap 5 | 1.5 Hour | 0 Min. | |
| Math | BPN | This week | 15 Min. | 0 Min. | |
| Math | BPN | Last week | 15 Min. | 0 Min. | |
| Math | BPC | Quiz #2 | 30 Min. | 0 Min. | |
| Math | BPC | Test 1 | 45 Min. | 15 Min. | |

## STEP FOUR: Final Calculation

On each line, add the **Human Factor** to the **Estimated Time** to get the **Final Calculation**. This is the amount of time you will need to allocate to complete the assignment on that line.

| Class | Activity | Chapter or Assignment | Estimated Time | Human Factor | Final Calculation |
|---|---|---|---|---|---|
| Eng | BPR | Chap 4 | 1 Hour | 30 Min. | 1.5 Hour |
| Eng | BPR | Chap 5 | 1 Hour | 30 Min. | 1.5 Hour |
| Eng | HW | Chap 4 | 1.5 Hour | 0 Min. | 1.5 Hour |
| Eng | HW | Chap 5 | 1.5 Hour | 0 Min. | 1.5 Hour |
| Math | BPN | This week | 15 Min. | 0 Min. | 15 Min. |
| Math | BPN | Last week | 15 Min. | 0 Min. | 15 Min. |
| Math | BPC | Quiz #2 | 30 Min. | 0 Min. | 45 Min. |
| Math | BPC | Test 1 | 45 Min. | 15 Min. | 1 Hour |
| | | | | **TOTAL** | **8 Hrs 15 Min** |

Now, prioritize the items in your table based on the degree of difficulty and deadline. Hint, place priority on the items you perceive to be more difficult.

## STEP FIVE: "Working it out!"

Now let's re-work your weekly schedule. Be sure not to change any of your highlighted **Non-Negotiable** items. These are the tasks that you must complete in order to not get further behind.

In the negotiable time slots of your schedule, find activities that you can temporarily give up until you are successfully caught up. Because you did not get behind in one day, **don't try to get caught up in one day and fall prey to the mentality of "THIS WEEKEND, I will get caught up" myth!** It is mentally overwhelming if you attempt to complete the entire 8.25 hours in one day. Instead, you should look for 1 - 2 hour openings in your schedule over multiple days. Activities are individually estimated so they can be easily "plugged" into the negotiable time slots on your schedule.

Use your discretion in deciding what you need to give up, but keep it real. Items that make good candidates are: social time, errands, and extra-curricular activities. Find and replace negotiable time in your week with catch-up activities from your table. If you simply cannot find enough time in a week (which is rare); you will need to stretch your catch-up period to two weeks. Follow your new schedule until you are caught up with the A+ PLUS Plan. Make adjustments to the schedule as necessary.

<u>**Write down your plan of action**</u> using the "Catching up without falling behind" Planner. Psychologically, you will be more committed to the plan if you write it down clearly and post the plan somewhere visible.

### Example of the Guaranteed A+ PLUS
### "Catching up without falling behind" Planner - Page 2

| Date | List of Activities | Time | Accomplished? |
|---|---|---|---|
| Monday | BPR - Eng Ch. 4 | 3–4:30 p.m. | Yes |
| Monday | BPN - Math – class 6 & 7 | 8:30–9 p.m. | Yes |
| Tuesday | HW - Eng Ch. 4 | 6–7:30 p.m. | |
| Wednesday | BPC - Math Quiz 2 | 5–5:45 p.m. | |
| Thursday | BPR- Eng Ch. 5 | 6–7:30 p.m. | |
| Thursday | BPC - Math Midterm | 6–7:00 p.m. | |
| Friday | HW - Eng Ch. 5 | 3–4:30 p.m. | |

As you can see from this example, this student wrote down a plan of action and had already accomplished Monday's tasks. As this student stays on this plan, she will be completely caught up by Friday at 4:30 p.m. This will allow her to fully enjoy the weekend without the dark cloud of "I need to catch up" hanging over her head.

### FAQ #19  I just learned the A+ PLUS Plan and I have a test this week; what can I do?

In an ideal world, students will learn the Guaranteed A+ PLUS plan prior to the start of an academic term. However, this is not a perfect world. Many students often do not learn about the A+ PLUS Plan until the middle of the semester. If you fall in this category and you have a test coming up within a week (or even tomorrow), here is the "quick and dirty" method for getting ready for a test!

**First, do BPN on the class notes.** When you can understand and BP the important concepts covered in class, you have a good foundation in preparing for a test. When you BPN for problem-based classes (such as math and science), pay special attention to HOW the teacher solved certain problems. This may give you an advantage on the test because you are gaining insight into the teacher's thinking. Many teachers want to see problems solved their way for ease of grading. By doing BPN, you are effectively reviewing in a productive fashion!

**Second, do BPC on corrected HW, quizzes or study guides (if applicable!)** BPC can help you get to the WHY behind the question, especially when your teacher has graciously assigned HW or given a study guide on the material covered on the test. If you understand the principles and concepts covered in homework or previous quizzes, you will be better prepared to solve the problems on the upcoming exam.

**Third, use TOH to get any questions answered and gain further insight from the teacher on how to prepare.**

### FAQ #20  If I have questions after reading this book, who can help me?

**You can register for FREE to become part of our web communities at www.NoMoreStudy.com.** There are postings on discussion boards and you will get notification for our regularly scheduled chat room Q & A sessions. The site also has a webpage where you can send us an email with your questions. You can expect an answer within 48 hours. We are serious about your academic success and you are not alone in this process!

# Appendix

# Blank Charts
# and Examples

## *Plan for Success*

| | Monday | Tuesday | Wednesday | Thursday | Friday | Saturday | Sunday |
|---|---|---|---|---|---|---|---|
| **6:00 AM** | | | | | | | |
| *6:30 AM* | | | | | | | |
| **7:00 AM** | | | | | | | |
| *7:30 AM* | | | | | | | |
| **8:00 AM** | | | | | | | |
| *8:30 AM* | | | | | | | |
| **9:00 AM** | | | | | | | |
| *9:30 AM* | | | | | | | |
| **10:00 AM** | | | | | | | |
| *10:30 AM* | | | | | | | |
| **11:00 AM** | | | | | | | |
| *11:30 AM* | | | | | | | |
| **12:00 PM** | | | | | | | |
| *12:30 PM* | | | | | | | |
| **1:00 PM** | | | | | | | |
| *1:30 PM* | | | | | | | |
| **2:00 PM** | | | | | | | |
| *2:30 PM* | | | | | | | |
| **3:00 PM** | | | | | | | |
| *3:30 PM* | | | | | | | |
| **4:00 PM** | | | | | | | |
| *4:30 PM* | | | | | | | |
| **5:00 PM** | | | | | | | |
| *5:30 PM* | | | | | | | |
| **6:00 PM** | | | | | | | |
| *6:30 PM* | | | | | | | |
| **7:00 PM** | | | | | | | |
| *7:30 PM* | | | | | | | |
| **8:00 PM** | | | | | | | |
| *8:30 PM* | | | | | | | |
| **9:00 PM** | | | | | | | |
| *9:30 PM* | | | | | | | |
| **10:00 PM** | | | | | | | |
| *10:30 PM* | | | | | | | |
| **11:00 PM** | | | | | | | |
| *11:30 PM* | | | | | | | |
| **12:00 AM** | | | | | | | |
| *12:30 AM* | | | | | | | |
| **1:00 AM** | | | | | | | |
| *1:30 AM* | | | | | | | |
| **2:00 AM** | | | | | | | |

## Sample Schedule #1: Regular Class Schedule

Extra-Curricular Activity: School Newspaper
Stress Management Activity: Playing Guitar

| | Mon | Tue | Wed | Thu | Fri | Sat | Sun |
|---|---|---|---|---|---|---|---|
| | Food / PH Bus to school | Food / PH Bus to school | Food / PH Bus to school | Food / PH Bus to school | Food / PH Bus to school | Sleep | Getting to Church |
| Period 1 | English | English | English | English | English | | |
| Period 2 | Spanish | Spanish | Spanish | Spanish | Spanish | Food / PH | |
| Period 3 | Physical Edu. | Physical Edu. | Physical Edu. | Physical Edu. | Physical Edu. | | Church |
| Period 4 | Math | Math | Math | Math | Math | Getting There | |
| Lunch | Lunch / Club meeting | Lunch | Lunch | Lunch / Club meeting | Lunch | | |
| Period 5 | Biology | Biology | Biology | Biology | Biology | | Getting home |
| Period 6 | Art | Art | Art | Art | Art | Volunteer at Local Soup Kitchen | HW - Math BPR - Math |
| 3:00-15 3:15-30 | Bus home | Bus home | Bus home | Bus home | Bus home | | HW - Biology HW - Biology |
| 3:30-45 3:45-4:00 | bpn-Eng./Span bpn-Math/Chem | bpn-Eng./Span bpn-Math/Chem | bpn-Eng./Span bpn-Math/Chem | bpn-Eng./Span bpn-Math/Chem | bpn-Eng./Span bpn-Math/Chem | | |
| 4:00-15 4:15-30 4:30-45 4:45-5:00 | Break Time (TV / Food, etc.) | Guitar Lesson | Break Time (TV / Food, etc.) | Break Time (TV / Food, etc.) | Guitar Lesson | Getting Home | play Guitar "me time" |
| 5:00-15 5:15-30 | HW - Math BPR - Math | HW - Math BPR - Math | HW - Math BPR - Math | HW - Math BPR - Math | Break Time (TV / Food, etc.) | play Guitar "me time" | Break Time (TV / Food, etc.) |
| 5:30-45 5:45-6:00 | BPR - Biology | BPR - Biology | BPR - Biology | BPR - Biology | | | |
| 6:00-15 6:15-30 6:30-45 6:45-7:00 | play Guitar "me time" | (Extra-Curr.) School paper Stuff | Dinner Getting to Church | (Extra-Curr.) School paper Stuff | play Guitar "me time" | House Chores | Dinner |
| 7:00-15 7:15-30 7:30-45 7:45-8:00 | Dinner | Dinner | Youth Group @ Church | Dinner | Dinner | Dinner | BPC - all HW - English BPR - Spanish |
| 8:00-15 8:15-30 | HW - Spanish BPR - English | HW - Spanish BPR - English | | HW - Spanish BPR - English | Free Time | Free Time | Free Time |
| 8:30-45 8:45-9:00 | Free Time | Free Time | Getting Home | Free Time | | | |
| 9:00-15 9:15-30 | | | HW - Spanish BPR - English | | | | |
| 9:30-45 9:45-10:00 | | | Free Time | | | | |
| 10:00-15 10:15-30 | PH / BED | PH / BED | PH / BED | PH / BED | PH / BED - ??? | PH / BED - ??? | PH / BED |

## Sample Schedule #2: Block Schedule

(Student was able to BPN during class time)
Extra-Curricular activity: Track and Field
Stress Management Activity: Jogging

| | Mon (A Day) | Tue (B Day) | Wed (A Day) | Thu (B Day) | Fri (A Day) | Sat | Sun |
|---|---|---|---|---|---|---|---|
| | Food / PH Getting to school | Food / PH Getting to school | Food / PH Getting to school | Food / PH Getting to school | Food / PH Getting to school | Sleep in & Watch Cartoons | |
| Block 1 | English bpn- English | US History bpn- history | English bpn- English | US History bpn- history | English bpn- English | | Church |
| Block 2 | Spanish bpn- Spanish | Computer bpn- computer | Spanish bpn- Spanish | Computer bpn- computer | Spanish bpn- Spanish | | |
| Lunch | Lunch (TOH-Art) | Lunch | Lunch | Lunch | Lunch | Lunch | |
| Block 3 | Art | Physical Ed. | Art | Physical Ed. | Art | HW & BPR for English | Lunch |
| Block 4 | Math bpn- Math | Chemistry bpn- chemistry | Math bpn- Math | Chemistry bpn- chemistry | Math bpn- Math | Break | Free Time |
| 3:00-15 3:15-30 | TOH- Math | TOH- History | TOH- English | TOH- Computer | Getting ready | HW & BPR for Math | |
| 3:30-45 3:45-4:00 | | | | | | | |
| 4:00-15 4:15-30 4:30-45 4:45-5:00 | Track & Field Practice | Track & Field Practice | Track & Field Practice | Track & Field Practice | Track & Field Tournament | House Chores | Jogging (My relaxing activity) |
| 5:00-15 | Getting home | Getting home | Getting home | Getting home | | Break | |
| 5:15-30 5:30-45 5:45-6:00 | P.H. Break (TV / food, etc.) | P.H. Break (TV / food, etc.) | HW & BPR for English | P.H. Break (TV / food, etc.) | | HW & BPR for Spanish | P.H. |
| 6:00-15 6:15-30 6:30-45 | HW & BPR for English | HW & BPR for Chemistry | Break | HW & BPR for Chemistry | Getting home | BPC - all Planning | Free Time |
| | | | HW & BPR for Math | | P.H. | | |
| 6:45-7:00 | Break | Break | | | | Dinner | |
| 7:00-15 7:15-30 7:30-45 | HW & BPR for Math | HW & BPR for History | Break | HW & BPR for History | Dinner | Free Time | |
| | | | HW & BPR for Spanish | | Free Time | | |
| 7:45-8:00 | | | | Dinner | | | Dinner & Family Night |
| 8:00-15 | Dinner | Dinner | | HW & BPR for Computer | | | |
| 8:15-30 8:30-45 | HW & BPR for Spanish | HW & BPR for Computer | Dinner & Family Night (Pizza & movie) | Chores | | | |
| 8:45-9:00 | Chores | Chores | | Free Time | | | |
| 9:00-15 9:15-30 9:30-45 9:45-10:00 | Free Time | Free Time | | | | | PH / BED |
| | PH / BED | PH / BED | PH / BED | PH / BED | | | |

## *"Catching up without falling behind" Planner A - Page 1*

| Class | Activity | Chapter or Assignment | Estimated Time | Human Factor | Final Calculation |
|---|---|---|---|---|---|
| | | | | | |
| | | | | | |
| | | | | | |
| | | | | | |
| | | | | | |
| | | | | | |
| | | | | | |
| | | | | | |
| | | | | | |
| | | | | | |
| | | | | | |
| | | | | | |
| | | | | | |
| | | | | | |

## *"Catching up without falling behind" Planner B - Page 2*

| Date | List of Activities | Time | Accomplished? |
|---|---|---|---|
|  |  |  |  |
|  |  |  |  |
|  |  |  |  |
|  |  |  |  |
|  |  |  |  |
|  |  |  |  |
|  |  |  |  |
|  |  |  |  |
|  |  |  |  |
|  |  |  |  |
|  |  |  |  |
|  |  |  |  |
|  |  |  |  |
|  |  |  |  |

## SEMINARS AND WORKSHOPS

Guaranteed 4.0 & Guaranteed A+ Plus presenters are available to facilitate customized learning seminars and workshops for various types of audiences. For more information, please refer to our website at www.Guaranteed4.com or call 972.236.5673.

## WRITE TO US

It is our mission to positively impact the life of every student who reads this book or attends the Guaranteed A+ Plus & 4.0 seminars. When you experience success in following the plan, we would love to hear from you. Please submit your testimonials via email to:

**Info@NoMoreStudy.com**
Re: testimonial

## ATTENTION: Civic, Professional & Educational Organizations

Quantity discounts are available on bulk purchases of this book for educational purposes, subscription/membership incentives, gifts, fundraising and reselling. Special books or book excerpts can also be created to fit specific needs. For information, please email us at:

**Info@NoMoreStudy.com**
Re: Bulk Purchases